THE SCHOLARSHIP SERIES IN BIOLOGY

General Editor: W. H. Dowdeswell

NEW CONCEPTS IN FLOWERING-PLANT TAXONOMY

NEW CONCEPTS IN
FLOWERING-PLANT TAXONOMY

By

J. HESLOP-HARRISON

WITH A FOREWORD BY

W. B. TURRILL, D.Sc., F.R.S.

Late Keeper of the Herbarium and Library, Royal Botanic Gardens, Kew

HEINEMANN

LONDON

Heinemann Educational Books Ltd

LONDON EDINBURGH MELBOURNE TORONTO
SINGAPORE JOHANNESBURG AUCKLAND
HONG KONG NAIROBI IBADAN

SBN 435 61390 1

First Published –	–	–	1953
Reprinted with Corrections –			1955
Reprinted with Corrections –			1960
Reprinted –	–	–	–	1963
Reprinted –	–	–	–	1964
Reprinted –	–	–	–	1967
Reprinted –	–	–	–	1969

Published by Heinemann Educational Books Ltd
48 Charles Street, London W1X 8AH

Printed in Great Britain by
Morrison & Gibb Ltd., London and Edinburgh

FOREWORD

By W. B. TURRILL, D.Sc., F.R.S.

Late Keeper of the Herbarium and Library,
Royal Botanic Gardens, Kew

ALL botanists must welcome this excellent account of
the impact of experimental and other intensive studies on
orthodox plant taxonomy. Dr. Heslop-Harrison has clearly
and very fairly summarised the results of a great deal of
modern research in the border belts between taxonomy,
ecology, and cytogenetics. Those of us who have pioneered
for modernisation of plant taxonomy by extending its aims
and methods, improving its descriptive matter, and enlarging
its concepts will be encouraged both by this book and by the
knowledge that the subject is attracting vigorous new recruits
of the calibre of its author.

In the development of such a subject as experimental plant
taxonomy we may expect, and, indeed, hope for, some
differences of opinion and emphasis. It is, for example, still
uncertain whether all that is discussed in this book will yield
results that can be assimilated by taxonomy. However, in
the past plant taxonomy has been adjusted to such changes
of outlook as those involved by a rejection of special creation
and acceptance of evolution. There is, therefore, good reason
to expect that it can and will be modified to absorb many
of the diverse data of the new systematics. Quite rightly,
taxonomists are, in some respects, conservative in accepting
every proposal made by experimentalists for reforming
their well tested systems. Not all that has the label "new
systematics" is new or systematics. Even cytogeneticists
and ecologists have been known to make mistakes, and they
do not always agree among themselves. One suggestion may
be made. Orthodox plant taxonomists (if there be any

nowadays) can better than most other botanists indicate groups that badly need intensive investigation by methods additional to those of the herbarium. There would be reciprocal advantages if experimentalists and their herbarium colleagues frequently consulted one another. This would, by introgressive hybridisation of methods and ideas, produce hybrid vigour in plant taxonomy.

CONTENTS

Chapter   *Page*

I.   INTRODUCTION: CLASSICAL TAXONOMY, EVOLUTION THEORY AND THE EXPERIMENTAL STUDY OF VARIATION   1

II.   THE PLASTICITY OF PHENOTYPES   13

III.   THE INTERNAL VARIABILITY OF POPULATIONS   27

IV.   ECOLOGICAL DIFFERENTIATION OF POPULATIONS   44

V.   GEOGRAPHICAL VARIATION AND REPRODUCTIVE ISOLATION   59

VI.   CYTOLOGY AND TAXONOMY   79

VII.   THE EXPERIMENTAL CATEGORIES   94

VIII.   THE RELATIONSHIPS OF "EXPERIMENTAL" AND "ORTHODOX" TAXONOMY   106

GLOSSARY   122

SUGGESTIONS FOR FURTHER READING   129

INDEX   130

ACKNOWLEDGEMENTS

I wish to express my thanks to Dr. W. B. Turrill, Director of the Herbarium and Library, Royal Botanic Gardens, Kew, and Mr. J. S. L. Gilmour, Director of the University Botanic Garden, Cambridge, for reading the manuscript of this monograph, and for much stimulating discussion of the topics surveyed in it. Thanks are also due to Dr. J. W. Gregor, Director of the Scottish Plant Breeding Station, Corstorphine, for permission to use his data and reproduce some of his diagrams. Some of the data and many of the remaining diagrams were provided by my wife, Dr. Yolande Heslop-Harrison, who is also responsible for the cover design. For her assistance in this and other ways I am most grateful.

To the Editor of this series of Biological Monographs I am indebted for his most helpful and detailed criticism of the manuscript.

J.H.-H.

May, 1953

CHAPTER I

INTRODUCTION

CLASSICAL TAXONOMY, EVOLUTION THEORY AND THE EXPERIMENTAL STUDY OF VARIATION

TAXONOMY may be defined as the study of the principles and practice of classification. In this general sense, it is concerned with a common and fundamental method of handling information of all sorts, biological and non-biological. However, it happens that the term was first introduced by the French botanist A. P. de Candolle in his "Théorie élémentaire de la botanique," of 1813, in a biological connotation, and through usage it has come to apply particularly to the methods, principles, and even in part to the results of biological classification. It is in this sense that the word is used in this monograph.

De Candolle's analysis of classificatory procedures in botany given in the "Théorie élémentaire" is of interest today as presenting a picture of botanical taxonomy as it looked to a great practitioner at the beginning of the nineteenth century. True to his training, de Candolle began his exposition of plant taxonomy by classifying methods of classification. He recognised the following:

Empirical classifications, "independent of the true nature of the object classified" (e.g. alphabetical classifications, where the order adopted is according to the initial letter of a purely arbitrary name);

Rational classifications, "having a real connection with the objects classified." These are further subdivided into:

Practical classifications, concerned with properties of plants mainly in relation to their value (or otherwise) to the human race;

1

Artificial classifications, designed primarily to facilitate the identification of unknown plants;

Natural classifications, giving expression to the true natural affinities between plants.

According to de Candolle, "rational" classifications were the only ones meriting serious scientific attention, and of these he considered "practical" classifications to be of minor importance. The "artificial" classifications of de Candolle's day were based exclusively upon the external form of plants, i.e. upon morphology. Their major groupings were based on one (or a very few) easily discernible characters, and the most successful systems were considered to be those which employed the most constant features and led most consistently to the correct identification of the plant under study. They had thus many characteristics of a "key" such as is to be found as an aid to plant identification in any modern flora— and in fact the arrangement adopted by Lamarck in his "Flore Française" of 1778 was the first example of the use on a large scale of what we would now call a dichotomous key. Several artificial systems had been proposed during the century prior to the writing of the "Théorie élémentaire," utilising all manner of morphological attributes of the vegetative and floral parts of plants. That which had attained the greatest vogue was the so-called "Sexual System" of the great Swedish systematist, Carolus Linnæus, in which flower structure was adopted as a primary basis of classification, with particular emphasis placed upon the number and distribution of stamens and carpels. The extraordinary popularity of the Sexual System arose partly from its own intrinsic merits judged in relation to the purpose for which it was constructed, namely, readiness of comprehension and ease of application. But it also came largely from the great personal authority of its author, whose prodigious systematic labours (and not least his rationalisation of nomenclature) had placed him in a dominating position both among botanists and zoologists from the middle of the eighteenth century onwards.

Linnæus's system adopted as its basic unit the *species*

which were grouped in *genera* after the manner which had already been regularised by the French botanist Tournefort. To Linnæus, as to many of his predecessors, genera appeared as "natural" units, comparable in this respect with the species of which they were composed. In the Sexual System, the genera were grouped simply by reference to a few floral characters. While many of the higher groups so formed appeared quite arbitrary, the genera composing others possessed in common many characters other than those used in the original classification. These groups seemed to possess an innate unity apart from that which had been imposed arbitrarily by the classificatory procedure—like the genera and species, they had the appearance of "natural" units. The existence of these systems of character correlation affected the thought of many naturalists, so that a concept of some form of "natural affinity" existing between plants became established. Quite early in his career, Linnæus came to accept that the ideal classification would be one which gave full expression to this natural affinity. In 1738 he published an account of sixty-five natural families, and a few years later he produced a "Fragmenta Methodi Naturalis," which was as far as the great master himself carried the task of constructing what came to be known as the "Natural System."

Lesser men of the post-Linnæan period were content to devote themselves to the description of new plants and to fitting them into the framework of the Sexual System, but others like de Candolle took up the challenge of the Natural System, and sought to establish sequences of affinities as a step towards its synthesis. These botanists rejected the idea that single characters chosen mainly for convenience could supply the basis for a perfect classification, and sought to produce groupings in which plants possessing the greatest number of common attributes were placed together. To achieve this, they came to insist upon intimate and detailed study, as far as was within their means, of every part of the plant, for only thereby did they believe that the true relationships and natural affinities could be exposed.

It is somewhat difficult for us today to imagine what sort of meaning these botanists who worked before the general acceptance of the idea of organic evolution attached to these concepts of "relationship" and "natural affinity." We must recall that at the base of most biological thought during the period lay the dogmas of the special creation and constancy of species, firmly stated by Linnæus and unquestioned by the majority of his contemporaries and immediate successors. To the systematists who were occupied with the description and cataloguing of the new plants and animals which were being discovered in ever increasing numbers as fresh parts of the world were explored, this was an article of faith of first importance. It is easy enough to see why it should have been: the fundamental unit of all systems of classification, of all description and illustration, was the species. To deny its existence, its constancy, or its permanency, was to strike at the foundations of all systematised knowledge of the living world. The essential character of the species, purely from the morphological point of view, lay in the similarity of all the individuals composing it and their dissimilarity from those of all other species. Nevertheless, other criteria were introduced by a few botanists, and the definition given by John Lindley in his "Introduction to Botany," of 1832, was essentially "biological" in character. Lindley wrote: "A species is an assemblage of individuals agreeing with each other in all essential characters of vegetation and fructification capable of reproduction by seed without change, breeding freely together and producing perfect seed from which progeny can be reared. Such are the true limits of a species . . ." The introduction of the idea of interfertility between members of the same species and, by implication, sterility between members of different species, gives this definition a strikingly modern ring.

While the doctrine of special creation was accepted by most of the systematists of the period, it did not so rigidly govern their outlook as is sometimes nowadays asserted. The internal variability of species was acknowledged, and was variously attributed to the diversity of circumstances under which individuals were cultured, to crossing and to "sporting." The observations of Lindley are illuminating in this connection: "It is probable in the beginning species only were formed, and that they have, since the creation, sported into varieties, by which the limits of species themselves have now become greatly confounded." The occurrence of intergradation between species was thus regarded as secondary, and in no way to be taken as evidence against their independent creation. Lindley found no inconsistency in stating in the same work: "Species are created by Nature herself, and remain always the same, in whatever manner they may be combined: they form the basis of all classification, and are the only part which can be considered absolute." From views like this sprang the "type" idea: that one individual could represent a species—an idea that dies hard even today.

Evidently, from Lindley's and similar definitions, the resemblance between individuals of a species was presumed to be due to "blood" relationship, but such could not exist outside the limit of the species. What then were the "affinities" discernible *between* species? There was only one logical view: if such affinities did exist between these independently created and reproductively separate lineages, they could only have been introduced as part of the plan of the creation itself. Thus an element of the *super*natural was introduced into the concept of the *Natural* System, a fact frankly acknowledged by some of its exponents.

As to the form the Natural System would take when perfected, i.e. how the major and minor groups could be disposed within it to indicate their affinities, the systematists of the early nineteenth century were rather vague. The early view of a regular succession of form from the simple to the more complex had already lost ground; Linnæus had used the simile of a geographical map, with states of different sizes distributed upon it, to express the type of relationship which he thought might exist; others the image of a net, and yet others that of a tree—although a tree somewhat different in its significance from that so favoured by the post-Darwinians. In any case, it was widely acknowledged that any presentation of the system on paper must necessarily involve falsification, since, as Linnæus had said, "mutual affinities exist on all sides."

Perhaps it was not so widely recognised that the form in which the variation of living organisms is represented in a classification must be to a large extent dictated by the nature of the taxonomic method itself. A hierarchical system of categories, in which the groups on each level are formed by placing together those of the level below, is fundamental to the taxonomic method. Such a system of categories had been established by Linnæus during the eighteenth century, one which in its essentials persists today. In Linnæus's system the Species formed the basic units; downwards they were divided, if necessary, into Varieties, whilst upwards they were grouped into Genera, Genera into Orders and Orders into Classes. Irrespective of how many intermediate categories are inserted, this method involves the establishment of discrete classes, and if what is being classified actually forms a continuum (i.e. a "spectrum" of variation with no actual breaks) these classes must be formed arbitrarily. Classification also demands a system of nomenclature, and the naming process itself can give an air of reality to units which have been defined arbitrarily in the first place.

Botanical nomenclature had in fact become stabilised in the latter part of the eighteenth century by the universal adoption of the binomial system. This system, in which a plant was given a name composed of the name of the genus plus a specific epithet indicating the species of the genus to which it belonged, was itself a reflection of the types of relationship which men had discerned between different kinds of plants. It was, in fact, an early application of the "hierarchical" idea, logical extension of which gives the pyramidal scheme of categories mentioned above. Foreshadowed in the works of the sixteenth-century herbalists, the binomial system was used extensively by the Swiss botanist, Kaspar Bauhin, in his "Pinax" of 1623, and finally established by Linnæus with the appearance of his "Species Plantarum," in 1753.

The primary aims of classical taxonomy were thus to describe and name all living species of plants, and to construct (or "discover" as some of the early botanists chose to put it) the Natural System. The framework into which it was to be fitted took the form of a hierarchy of categories, with a scheme of names for the groups in each rank. The methods by which the "relationships" and "affinities" were to be detected were primarily those of comparative morphology, and we owe to de Candolle in the "Théorie élémentaire" a penetrating analysis of how they were to be applied. All parts of the plant were to be taken into account, and attention was to be given to "estimating the relative importance to be attached to the various organs in comparison, to recognising the circumstances under which the true natures (homologies) of organs became obscured, and to evaluating the importance of the different points of view from which organs could be considered." De Candolle recognised and clearly stated the fundamental principle that a given structural plan can be adapted in different plants to various functional ends, and held that it should be the aim of the taxonomist to distinguish the underlying plan and utilise it in his classification rather than be led astray by functional adaptations. In particular he emphasised the manner in which the basic "symmetry" of organs could be obscured so as to make comparative studies difficult. He attributed this to three causes: abortion, degeneration and adherence. It is somewhat surprising that such dynamic concepts as these, each involving the idea of change from one state to another, can have been held by an upholder of the dogma of species constancy—and this de Candolle very definitely was. No doubt the contradiction was sensed by some of his contemporaries and immediate successors and led possibly to some speculation as to just how "fixed" species really were.

But it was undoubtedly the facts of "affinity" which had been uncovered in the search for the Natural System, as well as the questions raised by the mysterious concept of the system itself, which most helped to prepare the way for the acceptance by systematists of the idea of organic evolution. It is important to note that the aims and working techniques of classical taxonomy had been defined before the dawn of the evolution era. The product of the labours of taxonomists— the pattern of organic variation which they had begun to uncover—was an important source of factual evidence for the early proponents of evolution, used not least by Darwin himself. The doctrine of "descent with modification" provided the rational basis for the Natural System, but only after the latter had been conceived and partly constructed. As Darwin stated in the "Origin of Species," of 1859: " . . . community of descent is the hidden bond which naturalists have been unconsciously seeking, and not some unknown plan of creation. . . ."

Far from overthrowing immediately the structure of contemporary taxonomy, the doctrine of organic evolution thus provided a form of justification of its aims, and certainly a logical explanation for some of its results. To the post-Darwinians, the successful parts of existing classifications, those which best demonstrated "affinities," were to be interpreted phylogenetically, i.e. as being a form of representation of the facts of descent. So neat was this explanation of affinities that it was not long before certain systematists were claiming that phylogeny should be the *basis* of classification. Since without a reasonably full fossil record phylogeny cannot be positively determined, but can only be deduced from resemblances and differences observed among living organisms (which provide, of course, the real basis of "natural" classification), this is an excellent example of putting the cart before the horse.

In spite of the reasonable explanation it provided for some of the results of biological classification, the idea of organic evolution was in several ways in conflict with the practices of orthodox taxonomy from the beginning. Although it is true that men like John Lindley had cast doubts upon the "reality" of higher categories such as families and orders, the taxonomic hierarchy was tacitly accepted throughout the first half of the nineteenth century as a perfectly appropriate method of representing organic variation. This was in spite of the fact that, as we have seen, its structure was such as almost inevitably to introduce distortion unless what was being classified conformed to a pattern allowing clear sub-division at various levels and was also essentially static in character. Darwin's doctrine was implacably opposed to such an interpretation of natural variation, for although he was compelled to use "taxonomic" terminology in his exposition of the evolutionary idea and to talk of species, genera, families and the like in marshalling his evidence, he sought to show that the variability of the living world was essentially dynamic, and such as could not be contained adequately in any static system of categories. Furthermore, the special Darwinian doctrine of Natural Selection, which by him and many of his successors was often identified almost with evolution itself, had an important implication for taxonomy, for the logical conclusion of its teaching is that all evolution is progressive adaptation, and therefore that all the morphological differences between organisms discerned by taxonomists and used by them in the construction of classifications are no more than the by-products of the process of becoming better adapted.

Nevertheless, these discords did not immediately become apparent, and at first there seemed no reason for any alteration in either the aims or methods of taxonomy. The construction of a "natural" system of classification remained a primary task, and in fact there was increased justification for its pursuit, for the formerly esoteric concept of "natural affinity" could now be interpreted very satisfactorily in terms of phylogenetic relationship. Among higher plants, new sources of data to supplement external morphology had been found in the increasing knowledge of anatomy, and the important discoveries made in the middle of the century about the methods of reproduction in the Linnæan class of Cryptogams shifted the study of this group on to a new plane.

2

But these developments did not greatly affect taxonomic method. Throughout the plant kingdom, the techniques employed in classification, the categories and the system of nomenclature remained largely unchanged except for certain jugglings of the higher units in attempts to produce better "phylogenetic" groupings. Although the evolution theory quickly gained general acceptance, the doubts it threw upon the permanence of taxonomic units were not taken too seriously. After all, common-sense suggested that these were in any case permanent enough for all practical purposes. The more subtle implications in respect to continuity of variation, adaptation and the like, were mostly ignored by systematists, perhaps because they were not understood, but also no doubt because of their inconvenience. In fact, during the century-and-a-half after Linnæus, the taxonomic methods which he had so largely helped to establish were successfully employed with little or no modification to complete a major part of what might be termed the primary survey of the higher groups of the plant kingdom. Order was imposed where order had not been before, and to this extent the aims of classical taxonomy were achieved.

But the taxonomic procedure required that it should always be possible to distinguish "species," and although throughout much of the plant kingdom this had been facilitated by the actual existence of units which could be treated as such (i.e. groups of similar individuals separated from other such groups by clear variational discontinuities), it was inevitable, if Darwin's view of evolution had any relationship to the facts, that there would be a residue of variation which could not be satisfactorily dealt with in this manner. This proved to be so, for as floras became better known and their study passed over from the superficial stage to that of more critical analysis, "problem" groups were repeatedly encountered, and concentration on these led to the discovery of all manner of variational anomaly. Trouble arose again and again in the application of the old static species concept, and, in the plant kingdom, from a variety of sources. Some genera (e.g. *Rubus*, the blackberry genus, and *Hieracium*, the hawkweed genus) lent themselves to it well enough, but in these genera the description of species seemed to be never-ending, and as their numbers mounted into the thousands, more and more botanists began to have misgivings. On the other hand, other genera (e.g. *Salix*, the willow genus), remained refractory to a very large extent: only part of the morphological variability present in them could be satisfactorily disposed of by creating species; the remainder could not be fitted into any taxonomic straight-jacket.

Evolutionists had a ready enough explanation for many of the "critical" taxonomic groups: they were to be regarded as those in which evolution was currently active and the process of "speciation" incomplete. But this did not account for the differences between genera like *Rubus* and *Salix*, and as a matter of fact, these were not to be explained until well into the present century. Evolutionary theory, notwithstanding the new orientation it gave to biological thought, did not bring with it in the first instance any basically new research techniques. But the twentieth century saw the introduction of new experimental and observational methods of studying variation, methods which began to throw light on the actual mechanisms of evolutionary change.

Among the most important developments was the rediscovery of the "laws" of heredity, first formulated by the Bohemian monk, Gregor Mendel, in 1865, but unknown to the majority of biologists until 1900. This rediscovery led to the birth of genetics, and to a period of intensive investigation of the sources and mode of transmission of heritable variation. Then the growth of cytology, the study of the cell, revealed the importance of the cell nucleus as the actual seat of hereditary material, and correlation of genetical and cytological investigation placed new emphasis on the study of nuclear phenomena in relation to the variation of plants. Plant physiology, concerned primarily with function, inevitably began to throw light on the genesis of plant *form* as the phenomena of growth and development were explored.

Simultaneously, the new science of ecology placed stress on plants in their natural environments outside of the herbarium and laboratory, and so the study of morphological variation took on a new significance in relation to adaptation and survival.

The impact of the new sciences has been greatest in the lower categories of classification, for the facts they have brought to light concern, most immediately, natural variation at and below the level corresponding to the Linnæan species. Again and again the new lines of investigation have provided explanations for situations which had defeated the methods of orthodox taxonomy, but almost as frequently they have appeared to reveal the inadequacy of the existing taxonomic system as a means of expressing conclusions about the inter-relationships of plants. Cytologists, geneticists and ecologists, commencing perforce with the orthodox taxonomic units, have, as their work has progressed, repeatedly come to query the usefulness of these in expressing their findings.

Some workers have entirely rejected the basis upon which the orthodox taxonomic structure has been founded, and have constructed their own systems of categories of variation to express their findings, building up various "special purpose" classifications for the groups which have been studied experimentally.

And so has arisen the present situation, where the orthodox taxonomy of museums and herbaria, with its solid background of achievement in reducing to order so much of the plant kingdom, finds itself faced with the fact that experimentalists are on the one hand producing explanations for some of its oldest mysteries, and on the other condemning many of its traditional practices. The purpose of this short monograph is to trace some of the causes of this, and to show how the newer methods of investigating the variation of plants have simultaneously promoted the formation of new "taxonomies" while bringing about changes of viewpoint and technique in the old traditional taxonomy.

CHAPTER II

THE PLASTICITY OF PHENOTYPES

Genotype and Phenotype

THE basic element with which the taxonomist has to deal is the individual plant, and, for the sake of the present discussion, we may define this as one possessing physiological independence and lacking any form of living connection with others. What we can observe about the individual, its external morphology, anatomy, behaviour, functions—in fact the sum total of the attributes it reveals during its lifetime—constitutes the *phenotype*. Its innate genetical constitution, which is determined at the moment of fertilisation, is the *genotype*.

The genotype may be looked upon as comprising the hereditary material bequeathed to the individual by its ancestors, represented in the first instance by the two sets of genes present in the zygote, one set donated by each parent. The genes are carried in the chromosomes, which, through mitosis (somatic nuclear division), are duplicated accurately from cell generation to cell generation throughout the life of the plant, normally without change. As the result of chromosome duplication unaccompanied by cell division, certain mature cells of the plant body come to contain more than the two sets of genes present in the original zygote, but since the composition and balance is not altered, this fact does not basically affect the proposition that all the living cells of the plant are genetically equivalent, at least so far as the hereditary material residing in the nucleus is concerned. This constancy is not, of course, shared by the extra-nuclear cell components which participate in development and differentiation.

Through cell division, growth and differentiation, the zygote gives rise to the final many-celled organism. During this process, there is a constant interaction of the genes and the external environment, mediated by the cytoplasm. From the environment come the materials and energy with which the body is built, and the process of building is thus necessarily influenced by outside factors. These factors are subject to variation, and because of this, the form of the final product of the process of growth and development, the phenotype, is not fixed, like the genotype, at the moment of fertilisation. Under different environmental conditions, one and the same genotype may produce widely different phenotypes.

Now in constructing a classification of organisms, the taxonomist is concerned that it should have persistence in time beyond the life-span of the individuals he has available for study. Ideally, it might be thought that his ends would be best served by classifying genotypes. But all that can be investigated by the orthodox methods of museum and herbarium are phenotypes, and so the fact that one and the same genotypes in different environments may give rise to obviously different phenotypes assumes considerable importance. This is true for all biological taxonomy, but certain differences in the mode of growth of plants and animals make the problem rather more pressing for the botanist. In brief, these are such as to give plants a much greater degree of developmental plasticity than is possessed at least by the higher animals.

Developmental Plasticity of Plants and Animals

The growth of the higher animal tends to be determinate, or 'closed,' in the sense that an orderly and rather closely co-ordinated sequence of interlocked developmental processes occurs between the single-celled stage, the zygote, and the mature organism. If the individual is to survive and function normally, only relatively minor variations in the pattern of development are permissible. In contrast, plant growth tends to be largely indeterminate, or 'open;' the formation and development of organs is not concentrated in an early embryonic phase, but proceeds continuously. Only with the onset of the reproductive phase do we find closely integrated and determinate systems of organ-development at all comparable with those of animals, but even these are simpler and far less rigid, and the appearance of the primordia of the reproductive organs, following as it does at the end of a period of vegetative growth rather than occurring in an early embryonic stage, is itself conditioned by the previous experience of the plant. Visible vegetative growth consists of the increase in length and thickness of stems and roots, and the serial production of homologous organs conforming to a small number of patterns, while internally, cell differentiation leads to the formation of a range of tissues much more limited in their variety than those found in animals. The processes of cell division, growth, and differentiation are largely restricted to special areas, but in the case of perennials, these processes continue intermittently throughout life, and, perhaps because the internal environment is not so closely regulated in plants as in the higher animals, they are a good deal more susceptible to environmental influences. Accordingly, we find that many aspects of the external form of plants are governed closely by the conditions under which they are cultured, for the morphogenetic processes are more easily influenced from without than in the case of animals, and the looser organisation of the plant economy allows the potentiality of much greater variation of form without serious effects on viability.

Some of the consequences of the greater plasticity of plants are, of course, familiar to us all. We see nothing unusual in one of two trees of the same age possessing twice as many lateral branches as the other, but a healthy cat with eight legs would indeed be an object for a side-show. From the taxonomic point of view, the primary consequence is that many morphological features, including some of those which are most readily observable, have little or no value as indicators of genetical constitution and cannot be employed as criteria in any classification intended to have permanence.

We see thus that *selection* of criteria on which to base taxonomic divisions is essential, and that to make such selection it is of first importance to have some knowledge of the extent to which each of the characters available for study is subject to environmental control in its ultimate expression. Through experience, the skilled taxonomist comes to have an instinctive "feeling" for the probable relative values of characters, recognising and using in his diagnoses those which he terms "good" (because they are little modified by habitat conditions and thus provide a sound indication of genetical constitution) and rejecting those which he regards as "bad" (i.e. strongly affected by habitat conditions). But, strictly speaking, no form of observational technique can provide accurate information as to the relative plasticity of organs. Such can only be obtained by experimentation—by deliberate attempts to determine how one and the same genotype reacts in a variety of environments.

Naturally, the very features of the mode of growth of higher plants which make them specially susceptible to environmental modification help to facilitate experimentation of this type, since the fact that growth and organ-production are continuous processes means that the morphological reactions of the same individual can be tested in different environments. Three general types of procedure are available:

(a) varying the environment of the individual artificially in greenhouses or culture-rooms;

(b) simple transplanting, in which the plant is shifted bodily from one natural environment to another, and

(c) clone-transplanting, in which a single plant is split into parts which are then simultaneously each exposed to different environments.

The Effects of Single Factors

In wholly artificial environments, every external factor can be brought more or less under control, and the effects of the variation of any one or any group can be studied while the remainder are kept constant. This basic technique of plant physiological research has produced a great deal of data of direct interest to taxonomists. The morphological and anatomical repercussions which may result from relatively small and certainly non-injurious changes in the light environment may be taken in illustration. The *intensity* of illumination experienced by a plant affects the rate of stem elongation and ultimately internode length, branching pattern, and the size, position and posture of leaves. Pigmentation may be affected, and also other features such as stem and leaf anatomy, and the colour, texture and hairiness of aerial parts, all commonly included in taxonomic description. In Fig. 1 three leaves with short stem sections from corresponding parts of three plants of one and the same genotype of a *Rubus* species are illustrated. That in Fig. 1*a* has been grown in full light, that in Fig. 1*b* in medium shade, and that in Fig. 1*c* in deep shade. An outline drawing cannot do justice to all the differences which exist between these three, as for example in colour and texture, but it suffices to show that not only has size been affected, but also such features as hairiness, shape of stem section, and prickle form, all features regarded as important in *Rubus* classification.

Perhaps even more striking are the effects of changing the duration of the daily periods of light to which the plant is exposed, its *photoperiodic* environment. The subtle factor of day-length has a profound influence upon the whole life of the plants, ultimately affecting several morphological features of taxonomic significance. Length of day often decides the time of flowering, and even the number and kind of flowers produced. Its effects upon the vegetative parts of plants can be manifold, involving such features as absolute size, growth form, branching, stem anatomy, and the number, distribution, shape and structure of leaves, while furthermore it is often the principal factor governing the formation of vegetative organs of propagation and perennation—bulbs, corms, tubers and resting buds.

Much is known also of the morphogenetic effects of the experimental manipulation of other major factors of the plant environment such as temperature, moisture supply and mineral nutrition. But ultimately the taxonomist is concerned with the reactions of his material in nature, and the main value of experimental laboratory results to him is the aid they give in interpreting field phenomena. Even so, it is not always possible to assert confidently on the basis of laboratory experiment that any particular reaction in nature has a particular explanation, because in a natural environment the plant is exposed to the simultaneous variation of all or most factors, and under such circumstances it may be very difficult to interpret its reactions in terms of known responses to those factors varying singly. For this reason, information of more immediate value has often been sought through transplant experiments.

Transplanting Experiments

Simple transplanting experiments involve the transfer of the whole plant from one natural environment to another and the study of the resulting modifications. Such experiments suffer from certain methodological drawbacks, and also from the fact that the reactions of the plant to the second environment may be conditioned by its experience in the first, and direct comparison is not then permissible. Of more importance is the technique of clone-transplanting. This depends upon the power possessed by many plants to regenerate completely from small segments, which is the basis of vegetative propagation. The group of independent plants resulting from the splitting of a single "individual" forms a *clone*. Since all somatic cells can usually be taken to be genetically equivalent, the *ramets*, as the members of the clone are termed, form a group of plants all possessing the same genotype. If at the start of an experiment they are approximately the same in size, containing similar amounts of stored food, their morphological reactions in different environments can provide the type of evidence required—an indication of the kinds of phenotypes which can be produced by the same genotype in those environments.

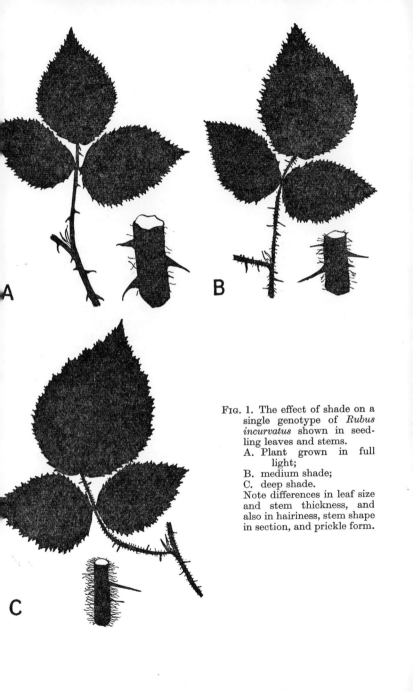

Fig. 1. The effect of shade on a single genotype of *Rubus incurvatus* shown in seedling leaves and stems.
A. Plant grown in full light;
B. medium shade;
C. deep shade.
Note differences in leaf size and stem thickness, and also in hairiness, stem shape in section, and prickle form.

So far, transplanting experiments have been mainly concerned with the effects of climate and soil, and those which have produced the most pertinent data have involved cultivation of the experimental material in prepared beds in different climatic zones or in different soils. Few have yet attempted to introduce biotic influences, although the effects on plant form of the very important ecological factor of competition undoubtedly require investigation.

The Experiments of Gaston Bonnier

The earliest clone-transplanting experiments on any extensive scale were those of the French botanist Gaston Bonnier, which were initiated in 1884 and finally reported upon in 1920. Unfortunately the conditions under which these experiments were conducted have been exposed to some criticism in that inadequate care is said to have been given to the essential matter of maintaining the purity of the cultures and to documenting continuously the changes in the transplants which took place over the long period of time involved. Nevertheless, Bonnier's techniques and conclusions are of interest, even although we may wish to accept some of the latter with reserve.

In the experiments which were commenced in 1884 in the Alps and in 1886 in the Pyrenees, Bonnier was concerned mainly with determining the influence of climate at different altitudes on the form and structure of various perennial plants. Transplant stations were eventually established at altitudes of 1,060, 1,900, 2,030 and 2,300 metres in the Alps, and at 740, 1,500 and 2,400 metres in the Pyrenees, and an attempt was made to eliminate soil influence by transporting the same soil to the various levels. In most of the clone-transplant experiments, perennial species were employed which occurred wild at the same levels as the transplant stations (or which had close relatives at those altitudes). Individuals grown at low or intermediate levels were cloned, and comparable ramets were planted in the culture gardens in the mountains and in the low-level garden near Paris. In a few experiments, segments of plants which had originated at high altitudes were transferred to low levels. The conditions at each of the transplant stations were maintained as far as possible in a natural state, and most of the beds were left unweeded.

Bonnier's reported results are both of ecological and taxonomic interest. He concluded that each species has a range of tolerance for climate within which it is capable of growing healthily and outside of which indefinite survival is not possible. In the case of the plants with which he experimented, this tolerance range corresponded more or less with the natural range. After transplanting from one part of the tolerance range to another, individuals underwent a process of morphological and physiological adaptation which took a period of time varying according to the species, complete adaptation being attained, for example, by *Galium verum* (the common ladies' bedstraw) in eight to ten years, but by *Juniperus communis* (common juniper) and *Calluna vulgaris* (heather) not for a period of over twenty-five years. In the case of the transplants from low to high levels, the important (and most controversial) point about the morphological modifications which took place was that they were claimed by Bonnier to be such as to make the transplanted individual *identical* in appearance and internal structure with forms occurring wild in the neighbourhood of the transplant stations, some of which had been previously given taxonomic recognition as varieties, subspecies, or even as separate species. Some seventeen cases of conversion of a low-level species into an alpine one were cited by Bonnier in his final report, including transformation of the common rockrose, *Helianthemum chamaecistus*, into the large-flowered alpine rockrose, *H. grandiflorum*; bladder campion, *Silene cucubalus*, into *S. alpina* and bird's-foot trefoil, *Lotus corniculatus* into *L. alpinus*. The modifications stated to be involved in these and similar transformations included striking changes in habit, usually towards "dwarfism" with more compact and more branched growth, and with more vigorous development of the subterranean parts. Leaves were reduced in size and became thicker and deeper green in colour, while flowers became larger and acquired more intense hues.

Transplanting experiments in North America

Similar conclusions to those of Bonnier were reached by the American ecologist F. E. Clements, following extensive transplanting experiments begun in 1901 at various altitudes on Pikes Peak in Colorado, and later in California. Using the techniques of simple and clone transplanting, Clements traced the adaptation of individuals of a very large number of North American species, mostly perennial herbs, to climates different from those in which they originated. Like Bonnier, he reported that the morphological and anatomical changes which ensued were such as to bring the transplants often into conformity with related subspecies or species occupying equivalent habitats in nature. He, too, claimed many startling conversions of one species into another, such, for example, as *Epilobium angustifolium* (common rose-bay willow-herb, or fireweed) into *E. latifolium*. Another extreme example is that of the genus *Mertensia*, in which Clements stated that four species, *M. pratensis*, *M. lanceolata*, *M. sibirica* and *M. alpina*, long recognised as distinct by taxonomists, were capable of complete or partial inter-conversion at will through manipulation of culture conditions.

Such extreme plasticity as this, affecting all parts of the plant, including those characters used as taxonomic criteria for the discrimination of species, would indeed have important implications for taxonomists were it general in the plant kingdom. However, the work of other investigators employing similar techniques, but equipped with a knowledge of modern genetics and perhaps more aware of the pitfalls in such experimentation, encourages a more conservative view. Clements's successors, working like himself under the auspices of the Carnegie Institute, have conducted over a period of thirty years a succession of transplant experiments over an altitude-transect from the Californian coast into the Sierra Naevda, and have interpreted their results very differently.

Their most significant findings relate to the genetical nature of altitudinal and other races, and as such they are discussed at length in Chapter 4. Here we are concerned with the fact that although these workers have fully investigated the type of morphological adaptation which commonly occurs after transplanting to new environments, they have failed to find evidence that altitudinal races are freely inter-convertible by manipulation of culture conditions, far less that any of the *species* they have studied can be so changed one into another.

The British Ecological Society's Experiments

While the more extensive programmes of transplanting experiments have been conducted to determine the effects on plant form of regional climates, others less elaborate but nevertheless highly significant have been concerned with investigating other factors, for example the influence of different soils. At the British Ecological Society's Research Station at Potterne in Wiltshire, Marsden-Jones and Turrill have conducted a series of experiments for a period of over twenty years to determine the effects on various native plants of differing soil conditions. The soils used included calcareous and non-calcareous sand, clay and chalky clay. In the majority of cases, clone-transplanting was employed, and data were recorded relating to performance, death-rate, flowering times and the like, as well as to morphological modifications. The results so far published indicate considerable differences in the capacities of the species tested to respond by change of form to soil influences. Thus the knapweed, *Centaurea nemoralis*, showed little morphological modification in the different beds, while the broad-leaved plantain, *Plantago major*, proved extremely plastic. The longer the period the ramets of this last species were cultivated on the different types of soils, the greater their degree of morphological divergence, differences appearing in such features as hairiness and time of flowering, as well as in habit and size of parts.

Aquatic and Amphibious Plants

The results of investigators who have tested the capacity of aquatic or amphibious flowering-plants to respond morphologically to environmental influences are of great interest, because they suggest that among higher plants, these are probably the most plastic of all. As long ago as 1902, Massart propagated vegetatively the same individual of *Polygonum amphibium* (amphibious bistort) on dry sand, moist soil and in water, and showed that in these different environments three very different phenotypes were produced which corresponded with forms occurring in nature which had been considered to merit separate taxonomic recognition. Glück, working in Germany, found that the heterophylly (possession of leaves of different shape and structure) of many water-plants was conditioned by the environment in which the leaves developed, i.e. whether at, above, or below the water surface, and that "land" and "water" forms of many amphibious plants, often very different in appearance from each other, were usually completely inter-convertible.*

Some Conclusions

From the results of the transplant experiments discussed above and others of a similar nature several generalisations can be made. Those which seem more or less non-controversial may be summarised as follows:—

   1. Through manipulation of the environment, changes can be brought about which affect to some extent every part of the plant and every function.

   2. Different genotypes differ in their capacity for reaction to variation in environmental factors: some show little powers of plastic modification of phenotype within their tolerance ranges; others are readily modified.

   3. Different organs of the same individual respond in

_____

*The great phenotypic plasticity of aquatic or amphibious flowering-plants (and also of certain ferns occupying similar habitats) is possibly connected with the fact that these habitats have been adopted *se ondarily* by plants already adapted to a terrestrial habitat.

different degree to changes in culture conditions; some show marked plasticity, others show little.

4. The vegetative parts of plants, in general, show the greatest capacity for response, and very frequently their responses are in the direction which gives the plant greater capacity for survival, i.e., they are directly adaptative in nature.

5. The reproductive organs of plants are, generally speaking, least subject to modification, particularly the basic floral features which have long been accepted as having the greatest taxonomic value—such as mode of insertion of floral parts, ovary structure and the like. On the other hand certain floral features *are* susceptible to modification, such as absolute size, pigmentation, and sometimes the numbers of parts, as, for example, the number of carpels in some Saxifrage species.*

6. Complete morphological adaptation of transplants may take a considerable period of time, but frequently modification begins quite rapidly, and is apparent in the first set of new organs produced after transplanting.

7. Changes produced in response to new habitat conditions are usually found to be reversed when the plant is moved back into its old habitat, but occasionally, particularly in the case of woody perennials, habit modifications imposed early in life may be largely irreversible. There is, furthermore, evidence that the previous experience of a plant may always to some extent govern its reaction in a given environment, so that plants of the same genotype may react in different ways to the same complex of environmental factors according to their individual previous histories.

From the above we can conclude that for a given genotype there is not one, but a range of environments in which successful development to maturity is possible, a range which we can

*It is, however, important to recognise that the physiology of reproduction is closely under the control of the environment in most flowering plants. External influences may decide whether flowers are produced at all, and if so, often their fertility and sex-balance.

conveniently term its tolerance. The phenotype produced may be different in structure or physiology according to the parts of the tolerance range in which it is partly or wholly developed, but the range of phenotypic expression is itself genetically determined, like the tolerance range, and may differ from genotype to genotype.

These concepts of "ranges" are, of course, largely abstract. Although we can define cardinal points within the tolerance range of a genotype, we cannot readily define that range itself in terms of physical factors. Because of the very large number of interacting variables involved, it is impossible to analyse plant environments completely in this way, and so it is impossible to predict (or for that matter to determine by experiment) what the reactions of a given genotype will be in every possible combination of circumstances. Correspondingly, no definite limits can be set to the phenotypic "plastic" range of a genotype; all we can do by experimentation is to establish certain points within it, and from these infer its general nature and extent.

CHAPTER III

THE INTERNAL VARIABILITY OF POPULATIONS

The Population Concept

EARLY systematists did not, of course, overlook the fact that the individual plant possessed a certain capacity for variation. Nevertheless, so long as the view was generally accepted that organisms were initially created in so many discrete and independent patterns, it seemed sufficient to assume that the description of even a single individual furnished an effective description of the species to which it belonged, provided that the individual chosen was "typical," and that attention was paid primarily to the "good" (i.e. more invariable) characters. There was further justification for this attitude in that most early taxonomists worked in temperate countries, and gained their knowledge of tropical and other relatively inaccessible floras mainly through casually acquired individual plants or parts of individuals. Nowadays, however, probably all taxonomists, irrespective of their views about the nature of species, would agree that this form of description is inadequate, and that ideally the description of all taxonomic units (or *taxa*, singular, *taxon*) should take into account the variation which exists between the individuals which compose them.

An effect of this change of approach is to throw emphasis upon the groups which individuals form in nature—upon *populations*. In a general sense, a population can be defined as an aggregate of individuals considered together because of some property or properties they share in common, as for example, the habitation of a given area at a given time. On this basis, population units can be defined on any level appropriate to the problem in hand and given such geographical or ecological significance as we may deem necessary. As a general term for these units, Gilmour and Gregor have introduced the word deme.*

In sexual organisms, as we shall see, the unit of greatest importance is the breeding population or *gamodeme*, which can be defined as that group of individuals which, because of their proximity in space and time, are potentially capable of interbreeding. Plants which habitually breed sexually are said to be *amphimictic*, and a population within which any individual is potentially capable of breeding with any other, or in genetical parlance, within which free gene-exchange is possible, is said to be *panmictic*. It has come to be generally accepted that the panmictic population is the unit of evolutionary change, and clearly if this is so, its properties are of basic importance to taxonomy.

However, before considering the types of variation encountered in populations of amphimictic plants, let us first examine the variation of those in which sexual reproduction is absent or plays a minor part.

Vegetative Reproduction

Vegetative propagation, whatever its form, serves to produce from the one individual, several possessing the same genotype and thus belonging to the same *biotype*. Theoretically at least, this process can go on indefinitely. Genetical variability does not appear in such a strain except with the relatively rare occurrence of somatic gene mutation, or until sexual reproduction takes place. The essential importance of the sexual process is that it allows the formation of fresh genotypes in the new generation through the segregation of the parental genes and their recombination in new patterns; with vegetative reproduction this does not take place.

*The "deme" terminology was introduced in 1939 as a general one to facilitate both taxonomic and genetical discussion. Suitable prefixes can be attached to denote specific types of deme, those originally suggested by the authors including: *gamodeme*, a deme forming a more or less isolated local intrabreeding population; *topodeme*, a deme occupying any specific geographical area; *ecodeme*, a deme occupying any specific ecological habitat. See also p. 105.

The various potato strains, the cultivated forms of many rosaceous fruit-trees and other horticultural plants illustrate the situation. It is the practice of the breeders of these plants to select suitable genotypes, characterised by producing phenotypes showing high yield, good quality, exceptional resistance to disease or other valuable properties, and to propagate them vegetatively in clones for the use of growers. Many such cultivated strains are heterozygous, and when allowed to reproduce sexually by seed the progeny is highly variable, rarely if ever reproducing the favourable gene-combinations of the parent. But in spite of the genetical heterozygosity, as long as vegetative propagation is continued, the strains tend to remain constant and invariable, expressing their favourable characters in each series of ramets.

In nature, clone formation by vegetative multiplication is not uncommon, occurring in many rhizomatous, stoloniferous and bulb-producing plants. In some species reproduction by special vegetative organs (propagules) is more frequent than by seed, as for example in the coral-root, *Dentaria bulbifera*, in this country. The specific epithet of this plant refers to its capacity for reproduction by bulbils. Vegetative reproduction is particularly frequent in aquatic plants. In various species of the pond-weed genus, *Potamogeton*, resting-buds at branch apices regularly become detached from the parental plant at the end of the growing season and sink separately to the pond bottom, where they germinate in the following spring to form a new group of individuals. Other water plants show a striking capacity for regeneration from fragments, and are propagated almost exclusively in this manner, being conveyed from pond to pond largely through the agency of water-fowl. The remarkable spread in Britain during the last century of the Canadian pond-weed, *Elodea canadensis*, is largely due to this faculty. Practically all the plants of this dioecious species in Europe are female, and since seed production in the absence of the male does not take place, the great majority probably belong to the same clone.

An interesting form of habitual vegetative reproduction

encountered in several genera is that known as *vivipary*, in which propagules resembling vegetative buds replace flowers in part or all of the inflorescence. This phenomenon is found in several families, but it is particularly frequent in the grass family, *Gramineae*, where it may be of adaptative value in some species living in extreme climates where the normal flowering process does not always lead to successful seed production. A common British example, to be found in many mountainous districts, is the viviparous sheep's fescue grass, *Festuca vivipara*, characterised by an "inflorescence" in which flowers are replaced by green plantlets.

The general term for those forms of reproduction which by-pass the sexual process (and thus prevent the segregation and recombination of genes which leads to the formation of new genotypes) is *apomixis*, and plants in which such a form of reproduction is more frequently adopted than the sexual are said to be apomictic. Examples of the types of apomixis mentioned above—those coming under the heading of vegetative reproduction—have, of course, been known to taxonomists for a great many years. Furthermore, there is little doubt that the implications of such happenings in connection with the pattern of internal variation of the species concerned have long been appreciated. No taxonomist has considered it worthwhile to give scientific names to all of the cultivated potato strains, even although they differ from each other in constant and often quite clearly discernible characters and exist in populations of thousands or millions, simply because it is widely appreciated that all result from the deliberate vegetative propagation of selected strains of the single species, *Solanum tuberosum*.

Agamospermy

However, the occurrence of another type of apomictic phenomenon in nature, until recently largely unsuspected, has led to a very great deal of taxonomic confusion and controversy, namely, the phenomenon of *agamospermy*. In agamospermic plants, the whole paraphernalia of sexual reproduction is present, and embryos and seeds are produced which function normally. But in various ways the essential processes of sexual reproduction—meiosis and fertilisation—are avoided, and the embryo is genotypically identical with its parent. Since seed formation without pollination was first observed at Kew by John Smith in 1841 in female plants of the dioecious Australian plant, *Alchornea ilicifolia*, agamospermy has been detected in some 75 genera of 35 families. The cytological mechanisms are highly diverse, and their details do not concern us here. The essential feature is that reproduction in these groups, while taking place by seed, is actually in most cases apomictic, and therefore all progeny arising from a common parent are genotypically identical.

The occurrence of agamospermy would cause little taxonomic difficulty were it the case that in any group it arose but once, and became permanent once established. Without doing violence to the basic category of the taxonomic hierarchy, the species, the biotype thus fixed could be defined and given recognition as such. But in many genera sexual reproduction does occasionally take place, and its result is to form a group of new biotypes, some or all of which are fixed and perpetuated as apomictic clones. Since constant (although small) differences can be detected between the biotypes, the critically eyed systematist can often recognise a high percentage of them wherever they occur in nature. They have, as a matter of fact, many of the desirable characteristics of the "classical" species—constancy, invariability and distinctness. But they differ from each other usually but minutely, they are often extremely local in their distribution, and their ranks are constantly augmented as fresh clones arise from chance sexual reproduction, through mutation, or, in some genera, through a form of internal gene-rearrangement known as autosegregation.

Biologically, these apomictically perpetuated biotypes can hardly be ranked with sexual species. Their special properties often make them of great phytogeographical and ecological interest, but the problem of how to classify them remains. A brief discussion of some treatments and suggestions is given in a later chapter; here it suffices, by citing the numbers of "species" which have been described and named in some common genera, to indicate the deep waters into which these apomictic groups have led taxonomists who have attempted to apply to them the orthodox methods. In the hawthorn genus, *Crataegus*, in North America, some 1,100 forms have been described as species; in the blackberry genus, *Rubus*, in north-western Europe, over 4,000, and in the hawkweed genus, *Hieracium*, perhaps over 10,000. It is hardly necessary to say that the number of botanists who have acquired familiarity with these groups sufficient to operate the cumbersome system of nomenclature these figures represent is small indeed!

Self-Pollination and Cleistogamy

While not a form of apomixis, another type of reproduction is encountered in the higher plants which may produce similar results in that it occasionally leads to the establishment and perpetuation of populations consisting of single biotypes. This is reproduction involving persistent self-fertilisation. Such a form of reproduction tends in a few generations to reduce heterozygosity to small proportions, so that the processes of meiosis and syngamy no longer serve to produce fresh genotypes, but only reconstitute that of the parent. The population then comes to consist of an assemblage of pure-breeding biotypes or "pure lines," as was first found, by the Danish geneticist Johannsen, to be the case in the cultivated bean variety, Princess. Many instances of the habitual self-pollination of some of the flowers produced each year are known in wild plants, familiar examples occurring in the violet genus, *Viola*, in which, after the appearance of the flowers which are open to cross-pollination, others are produced which do not open and which produce seed after internal pollination (and are said, therefore, to be *cleistogamous*). In a great many other species self-pollination is indeed frequently an alternative to cross-pollination, acting as an insurance against its failure. It is complete (or *obligate*) self-pollination, however, which is likely to have taxonomic repercussions, since as we have seen it may lead to the establishment of local populations consisting of one or a few biotypes. As in genera in which apomixis occurs, these because of their constancy and distinctness have acted as a constant temptation to botanists adhering to the classical concept of the species. An interesting example in the British flora is found in the helleborine-orchid genus, *Epipactis*, where certain populations, probably originating from the widespread, polymorphic, cross-pollinated *Epipactis helleborine*, have become obligately cleistogamous or habitually self-pollinated, and have developed distinctive local races which, from the small amount of internal variability which they show, seem to consist only of one or a few biotypes. Some half-dozen of these have been described as species and given binomials in Britain alone. The constancy of the cultivated varieties of the temperate cereals, wheat, barley and oats is similarly due to habitual self-pollination.

Variation in Non-Sexual Populations

It follows from what has been said in the previous chapter that under uniform conditions of growth all members of a population of the same biotype should be phenotypically identical. This has been demonstrated in experiments in growth chambers when close control of light, temperature, humidity, air movement, root moisture and nutrition has been established. Under these conditions, peas and other plants of genetically almost homozygous strains show remarkably uniform behaviour in growth, organ differentiation and development.

In natural habitats, the variability of individuals belonging to the same biotype will obviously arise from the differential action of environmental factors upon them during growth. The types of phenotypic modification produced by extreme differences of culture conditions have already been discussed; here we are concerned with the variation between individuals likely to be encountered in a population occupying a natural habitat of reasonable ecological uniformity. Obviously some differences will be due to differences in age of individuals. But between individuals at the same stage of development, small dissimilarities are likely to develop as a result of the fortuitous operation of innumerable minor factors—factors which probably would be beyond analysis in detail, like seed posture, root competition and leaf shading, some of which might operate in any one plant in one direction, and in others, in another. We might justifiably expect, then, that in any large enough population the variation between individuals for many quantitative features like stature, weight or leaf area would tend to be continuous. This is, in fact, found to be the case. The problem is how, in defining such a population, can continuous variation of this sort be taken into account?

An obvious approach, and one which has formerly been commonly adopted in defining, for example, the variation to be expected in a *Rubus* biotype, has been to state for the attribute under consideration a range within which plants may be expected to vary. Although this method may be the only possible one when only a limited number of specimens is available, say in purely herbarium studies, it has little to commend it, since the range will itself depend upon the number of individuals examined, and in any case, a statement of the extremes gives little information about the actual structure of the population.

It is here that statistical methods become of value to taxonomy. In a population of the type we have just been discussing, the manner in which an attribute, such as a particular dimension of an organ, varies quantitatively can be represented graphically by dividing the observed variation range into intervals of convenient size, striking off a corresponding number of intervals along the horizontal axis and erecting vertical columns of a height proportional to the number of individuals falling within each. Such a graph is known as a histogram, and an example showing variation in width of largest leaf in a sample from a population of an apomictic biotype of dandelion, *Taraxacum officinale*, is reproduced in Fig. 2A.

It will be seen that a polygon could be produced by joining the midpoints of the vertical columns of the histogram, and if the number of classes and the number of individuals measured were made very large, this polygon would tend towards a smooth curve of characteristic form, known as the *normal curve*. That this is the case is largely a matter of empirical observation, but that it should be so can be argued from the theory of probability, from which the normal

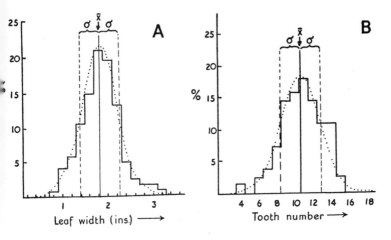

Fig. 2. Histograms showing variation in a colony of *Taraxacum officinale* agg., the common dandelion. The histogram shows the percentage, of a population sample of 200, falling in each class, and the dotted line is the normal curve giving the best fit to the sample data.

A. A "size" character, maximum width of largest leaf.

B. A "meristic" character, number of teeth on the margin of the lowest complete lobe of the largest leaf.

$\bar{x}$ marks the mean of the sample for each character, and the standard deviation is set off as the distance σ on either side of the mean.

distribution is itself deduced. The normal curve is symmetrical and any particular example can be defined completely by two constants, the mean ($\bar{x}$) which places the centre of the distribution, and the standard deviation (σ) which is a measure of the width of the curve, or dispersion, being actually the distance from the mean to the points of inflexion of the curve on either side. From a succession of measurements of any quantitatively varying attribute taken from the individuals of a population it is a relatively easy matter to calculate values for $\bar{x}$ and σ which define the normal curve which gives the best fit. If this form of distribution actually prevails in the population, or if it is fairly closely approached, then these constants provide the best method of summing up concisely all that is known about the variation in it of the particular attribute under study. In Fig. 2A, the normal curve which gives the best fit to the data has been superimposed. It will be seen that it provides a very good picture indeed of the variation.

Within a genetically homogeneous group such as that we have been discussing, environmental influences are not only likely to produce continuous variation in the sizes of organs, but also in other features such as colour, hairiness and the like, which, while not so readily assessed in numerical units as size or weight, may nevertheless be considered to vary continuously in that distinct grades separated by discontinuities cannot be recognised. In these features frequency distributions again tend to approximate to the normal curve. In contrast with this type of variation is that shown by such characters as petal number and leaf number, where the variate can assume only integral values, i.e. be represented by whole numbers, since the organs concerned must either be present or absent. This type of variation is termed *meristic*. If, in dealing with a case of meristic variation, a reasonably large number of values is possible, and if the average number is not very small, it is commonly found that the normal curve provides a good enough fit both for description and comparison. This can be seen from Fig. 2B, which is a histogram showing the variation in tooth-number on part of the leaf in the same sample of a dandelion biotype as is treated in Fig. 2A.

Variation in Sexual Populations

In an apomictic population, the biotypes have continuity in time since their genotypes are not broken up and reassembled in each generation, but handed on intact. Genetically, the situation is essential static; it may be represented diagrammatically as in Fig. 3A.

The essence of the sexual process in habitually outbreeding plants is that through the gene segregation and recombination which it involves, it brings about a continuous substitution of genotypes from generation to generation. In effect, what takes place in each generation in a population of outbreeding individuals is that the entire genetical material of the population is reshuffled: if biotypes present in the previous generation reappear, it is because chance has brought together again identical gene-combinations. In an amphimictic population which is maintaining constancy of numbers, on the average each individual of each generation will have had two parents in the previous and will be one of the parents of two individuals in the next. Since breeding is random, the situation is dynamic and may be represented as in Fig. 3B. In a population in which reproduction is sometimes sexual and sometimes vegetative, an intermediate situation prevails which can be represented as in Fig. 3C.

One important point about the panmictic population is that whereas as far as individuals are concerned there is continuous genetical change, the average structure of the population as a whole may show greater stability over a period of time. The total amount of genetical variability in a population depends firstly on the number of allelomorphs at each locus of the haploid genome present in it, and secondly upon their proportional representation. The former can be changed only through gene mutation or loss, and it can be shown mathematically that in large populations the latter tends to remain constant in time unless under the prevailing

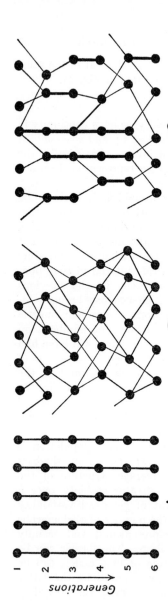

A. Population which is obligately apomictic. The lineages are separated and unchanging from generation to generation (this could also represent the result eventually produced by continuous self-pollination).

B. Population which is obligately amphimictic. Each genotype persists through one generation only and on the average each individual is parent to two others in the following generation. The different biotypes have no continuity, but the average structure of the population remains much the same.

C. Population in which reproduction is sometimes sexual and sometimes not. Some biotypes persist through a few generations, but gene segregation and recombination occur at intervals whenever sexual reproduction takes place.

Fig. 3. Diagrammatic representation of different types of breeding system in plants. For simplicity, it is assumed that annual species are concerned, and the course of breeding through six years is represented. The black dots represent individuals; the heavy lines, reproduction which does not involve a sexual process, and the thin lines, sexual reproduction.

environmental conditions certain genes or combinations of genes reduce the capacity for survival of the biotypes in which they occur relative to others.*

It is this concept of the statistically predictable population composed of evanescent individuals, all linked with each other genetically through ancestry and all potentially capable of becoming linked again through their descendants, which has come to occupy a central position in modern evolutionary thought. As already suggested, taxonomists, as students of the end-products of evolution, are now becoming impelled also to accept the population as the biological unit in sexual organisms and to transfer to it the attention formerly given to the individual.

The most striking form of internal variability encountered in natural populations is that known as *polymorphism*, in which two or more distinct forms occur side by side. Dioecism (distribution of male and female flowers on different plants) and polyoecism (occurrence of unlike sex-combinations on different plants) are examples of polymorphism, but examples of a special type since the presence of two or more sex-forms in a population is obviously connected with the breeding-system prevailing in it. Similarly, heterostyly, the condition found, e.g. in the common primrose, *Primula vulgaris*, and purple loosestrife, *Lythrum salicaria*, in which different plants in the same population produce flowers with different dispositions of the stigmas and anthers, is a form of polymorphism connected with the breeding behaviour of the population (actually it serves as a mechanism to promote cross-pollination) and is therefore in a special class. But polymorphism not connected immediately with the breeding system is almost as common. Flower colour and pattern variation provides an obvious case, such as is found for example in the foxglove, *Digitalis purpurea*, some populations of which contain more white-flowered plants

*In small populations other conditions may prevail, for it may be possible for a particular gene to be fixed and its allelomorph lost purely through chance. Small isolated populations can thus show genetical "drift" without any environmental selection, a phenomenon termed the Sewal lWright effect.

than "normal" purple ones. The origin of such polymorphism may be relatively simple genetically, depending on one or a few pairs or series of allelomorphs having large (i.e., "obvious"—although physiologically they may be really quite minor) individual phenotypic effects. Taxonomically, clearly distinguishable variants of a non-sexual type have been commonly treated as "varieties" or "forms." However, if we wish to extend the study of such polymorphism beyond merely initial description and classification, it may be important to establish the proportional representation of the variants throughout the species area, which can be done by estimating their representation in whole colonies or in large samples of them.

It is commonly found that in a given habitat differences between biotypes range from those which are clear cut, giving the type of polymorphism discussed above, to those in which the classes cannot readily be distinguished by eye. In the latter case the variation between individuals of the same biotype due directly to slight differences in their conditions of growth may obscure any variational gaps between the biotypes, so that the variation appears continuous in the population as a whole.

These considerations suggest that in actuality the hereditary basis of quantitative variation is in no way fundamentally different from that underlying polymorphism, but simply that more genes are involved, all affecting the same phenotypic character but all with small individual effects. Such complementary genes are known as *polygenes*. Since members of polygenic systems segregate separately and recombine following the same laws as other genes, their distributions in panmictic populations tend to be random. To see how this governs quantitative variation within the population, let us assume that the feature concerned is leaf size, and that it is controlled by three genes all essentially similar and complementary in their effects. The "+" allelomorphs make for large size, the "—" allelomorphs for smallness. The smallest-leaved biotype will obviously be that in which all six genes of the genome (three in each haploid chromosome set) are "—", while the largest leaves will belong to that in which all are "+". But if the allelomorphs are scattered at random in the population in approximately equal numbers, the number of genotypes in which these extreme combinations will occur will be small—in fact, in this case, each in less than one in sixty. The most frequent class will be that in which three "+" occur with three "—", which will phenotypically mean intermediate leaf size. On either side of this modal class, the numbers with more and less favourable combinations will fall away towards the extremes. Such a distribution will no doubt have a familiar sound to the reader: it is, in fact, an approach to the normal curve discussed on p. 35, and as the number of gene-pairs involved in such variation becomes greater, the conformity with normal distribution increases.

Thus in an outbreeding population, genetically based continuous variation is, in the same way as that arising from environmental causes, often of a form which can conveniently be summed up by fitting a normal curve. In fact, the variation arising from the two sources, heritable and non-heritable, is combined in the observed phenotypic variation, and there is no way of separating the two components, or of deciding which is the more important, except through experimentation.

An example of continuous variation in a linear dimension in an outbreeding population is given in Fig. 4A, which is a histogram showing the distribution of the length of the flower nectar tube or "spur" in a large sample from a colony of the common spotted orchid, *Orchis fuchsii*. That a similar sort of distribution is found in a meristic character is shown by Fig. 4B, which illustrates the distribution of numbers of leaves per plant for the same sample. In each case, a normal curve provides a reasonably good fit to the data.

Conclusions

Perhaps the most important general conclusion to be drawn from what has been discussed in this chapter is that the

4

breeding system prevailing in any group of plants is always of enormous taxonomic importance, for it is the breeding system above all factors which governs the pattern of group-variation. Strictly, breeding systems can only be investigated fully by experimental means, but sufficient has been said to show that the results of certain aberrations like apomixis are so distinctive that their presence can be foretold with assurance even without experimental tests.

It will also be evident why attempts to apply a rigid species concept based upon the meticulous description of "type" individuals produced such diverse results in different genera. The description of individual biotypes in *Rubus*, although

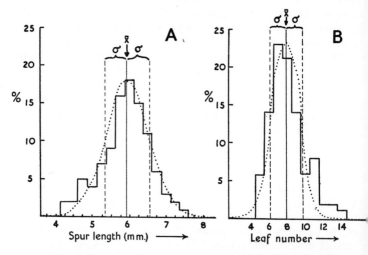

FIG. 4. Variation in a colony of the spotted orchid, *Orchis fuchsii*, a sexual species. As in Fig. 2, percentage is shown in each class, and the normal curve giving the best fit to the sample data is indicated.

    A. A "size" character, length of flower "spur" (i.e., the nectar tube at the base of the largest petal).

    B. A "meristic" character, number of foliage leaves per plant.

$\bar{x}$ marks the mean of the sample for each character, and the standard deviation is set off as the distance σ on either side of the mean.

apparently a never-ending task, at least served to define entities which appeared to have reality and independence over a period of time extending through many generations. The same method applied to certain critical sexual genera, like *Orchis* and *Salix*, was very much less successful, simply because of the impermanence of biotypes in such genera and the fact that they are independent only during the life-time of the individual, representing, as it were, knots in a net stretching through time. The unit of study in these genera has to be the population, i.e. the net, not the knot.

But even this transfer of emphasis does not solve the "species" problem for the taxonomist. Few species indeed consist of a single panmictic population isolated from all others reproductively and morphologically, or even of a number of such populations all showing similar biotype composition. Most are composed of numerous segments wholly or only partially separated from each other, and between those segments there is commonly morphological and physiological variation.

CHAPTER IV

ECOLOGICAL DIFFERENTIATION OF POPULATIONS

Experimental Cultivation as a research Technique

In Chapter II mention was made of the work of Massart, who found that *Polygonum amphibium* when cultivated on dry sand, moist soil and in water produced three distinct phenotypes. From his experimental results, Massart concluded that corresponding forms in nature had arisen in a similar manner through direct modification by environment. Were this so, it would provide an example of the morphological differentiation of populations by habitat-modification of genetically uniform original stock. But as the Swedish botanist, Turesson, pointed out in 1922 at the beginning of his own studies on the differentiation of plant populations, Massart's experiments *prove* nothing of the sort. The three forms of *Polygonum amphibium* found in nature may be no more than modifications of similar genotypes, or they may possess dissimilar genotypes, differing from each other in genes concerned with physiological and morphological adaptation. From the mere inspection of phenotypes there is no way of discriminating between true genetical difference and simple environmental modification.

One way open to have proved (or disproved) Massart's contention would have been to have cultivated plants of the three forms, taken from nature, side by side in a common neutral habitat. Morphological convergence would then have been strong evidence in favour of his suggestion, which could finally be proved by a demonstration that all three forms could be inter-converted by "reciprocal" transplanting. Failure of the transplants to converge in a neutral habitat would suggest that the forms might be genetically dissimilar, and a demonstration that the progeny of the three were not alike, even when grown from seed in the same habitat, would provide further evidence of genotypical difference, which could be finally established by crossing experiments.

Experimental cultivation is thus a technique of importance not only in exploring the phenotypic plasticity of single genotypes, but in detecting differences between genotypes. The essence of this was appreciated by de Candolle, who advocated the cultivation of critical forms side by side in various soils to see whether or not their differences would eventually disappear. Rather more than a century ago, A. Jordan used this method of comparative culture to distinguish between hereditary and non-hereditary forms in a great many species of the French flora. Jordan sought to demonstrate that the Linnæan species (subsequently called "Linneons" by Lotsy) were often large aggregates which could be broken up into minor units which were "perfectly limited and distinct, constant and invariable in their differences," which he took to represent the real species. As might be expected, what Jordan often succeeded in defining were individual biotypes possessing distinctive characters, owing their perpetuation to reproductive peculiarities. Thus the spring whitlow grass, *Erophila verna*, was pulverised into more than 200 "species" ("Jordanons"), many of which are now known to be obligately self-pollinated pure-lines. In outbreeding species Jordan was less successful in defining permanent or even persistent forms, many of those he described being simply biotypes with distinctive character combinations, sorted out fleetingly from the flux of forms occurring in wild populations.

It was Göte Turesson who pioneered the use of the technique of experimental cultivation for the investigation of the genetical differentiation of populations, and brought into prominence what has now come to be known as "experimental taxonomy." From the outset of his studies, Turesson was concerned with the relationships between the genetical composition of populations and their environments—with what he termed the *genecology* of plants. He noted, as had Gaston Bonnier and others before him, that the majority of species possessed ranges which extended through diverse climatic zones and often through several different types of habitat, and that populations occupying ecologically different parts of the range commonly showed physiological and morphological peculiarities which were often of an adaptative nature.

Turesson's original experiments were aimed at the investigation of the basis of these differences: whether they were in fact the outcome of direct plastic modification of similar biotypes in each divergent habitat, or whether they were due to actual heritable differences between the populations. The plants he studied were from the flora of southern Sweden, selected because of their commonness and their occurrence in a wide variety of habitats. The methods he adopted were those of comparative cultivation. Samples of several plants were collected at random from each population and transferred to the experimental garden at Åkarp in south-western Sweden, where those from the various sources were cultivated under uniform conditions. The progress of changes in morphology and behaviour, if any, were followed over several years, and after protracted periods of culture, any residual differences were noted which seemed to indicate genetical dissimilarity.

Genetical Adaptation and the Ecotype Concept

Some actual examples may be taken to indicate the type of results which Turesson obtained. Yellow loosestrife, *Lysimachia vulgaris*, occurs in moist alder swamps in southern Sweden in a tall, attenuated form with large thin leaves and other characteristics of the sort common to plants living in shade. After two years' cultivation, it came to correspond in all essentials with the ordinary meadow or fen form. From this, it was concluded that the alder-swamp form tested was no more than a modification of the ordinary: a result of a similar type to those reported by Gaston Bonnier in his Alpine and Pyrenean transplant experiments.

But results of this nature were quite exceptional in Turesson's work. Generally speaking, he found that the differences observable in the field between populations of species occupying very diverse habitats tended to be maintained in the Åkarp garden (although often not in such extreme forms) and that they were therefore to be interpreted as indicating actual genetical distinction. An excellent example is that of the hawkweed, *Hieracium umbellatum*. This is one of the few sexual species in the predominantly apomictic subgenus *Archieracium*, and it occupies a wide range of habitats in southern Sweden, showing great variability. Turesson was able to demonstrate that the differences in appearance and behaviour of different populations persisted in culture, and he grouped the forms occurring within the quite limited area he investigated into five general types, two occurring in sandy soils (one on shifting dunes, the other in sandy fields and fixed dunes), two on sea cliffs (east and west coast) and one of open woodland. These types differed from each other in stature, habit, leaf size, shape and anatomy, inflorescence shape, flowering period and in powers of shoot regeneration. Proof that these differences were hereditary was obtained by showing that they were expressed in plants grown from seed in the culture garden.

Even when judged simply from an anthropocentric point of view, certain characters shown by the different habitat-races of plants like *Hieracium umbellatum* were apparently adaptive. For example, prostrate growth habit, while general in plants growing in sandy meadows and fixed dunes, would appear to be disadvantageous among shifting dunes, where the prevailing type was found to be erect and capable of rapid shoot regeneration, properties which might be expected to protect it from being killed by blown sand. But as Turesson pointed out, adaptation is likely, in general, to be a much more subtle matter, and to be bound up with the total reaction of the genotype, even although certain specific attributes such as growth form may be of greater importance than others.

Two questions of general importance arose from these early experiments: firstly, how did populations occupying different habitats become differentiated genetically from one another; and secondly, why was genetical adaptation found at all when many of the plants concerned were capable of producing modified phenotypes which were similar to the genetical forms and were apparently equally capable of occupying specialised habitats. Turesson's answer to the first was that the specialised habitat races arose through "the genotypical response of the species population" to the differential habitat factors. By this he implied, that from the flux of biotypes which constituted the general species population, that group whose special properties fitted them to existence in the specialised habitats migrated out and colonised those habitats wherever they were encountered. For the product of this genotypic response to habitat, Turesson proposed the term *ecotype*. Obviously, if ecotypes represent groups of biotypes selected from the general species population because of their capacity for growth in specific habitats, they should be capable of polytopic origin: i.e. they should be differentiated out anew wherever the general species population migrates into an area where the differential selective habitat factors operate. This view was upheld by Turesson, who pointed to the fact that the dune populations of *Hieracium umbellatum* in the different coastal areas of southern Sweden, while similar in gross morphology, differed from one another in minor, presumably non-adaptative, leaf characters. These leaf characters could be correlated with those of neighbouring inland types, suggesting that the biotype complexes in each dune system had arisen independently from the local inland species population.

The second question, as to why genetical adaptation of populations to extreme habitats should be more often encountered than mere plastic modification of individuals, is a more subtle one. Turesson's view was that the capacity for plastic modification may sometimes be a questionable asset, and that so much may be demanded from the plant in making the modification that the factors that brought it about could be looked upon as limiting general development. On the other hand, such limitation is not imposed upon a plant which produces the appropriate adaptive form without the compulsion of external influences. Stated differently, we may suppose that physiological economy in adaptation has itself selective value. A cognate viewpoint has been developed more specifically by Waddington, who has pointed out that if there is genetical variability in a sexually reproducing population in the readiness with which a plastic change is produced, selection will necessarily favour those individuals which the more readily acquire the modification should it be of selective value. Over a number of generations, gene complexes may thus be assembled which establish the appropriate developmental path without severe environmental coercion; the acquired characteristic will have become genetically assimilated.

A result of Turesson's with the devil's-bit scabious, *Succisa pratensis*, is interesting in connection with these speculations on the replacement of "ecad"* by "ecotype". Dwarf forms of this species occur frequently in the upper parts of salt-marshes in Scandinavia, and when these were transplanted to the experimental garden, it was found that all increased their size to some extent in two or three seasons. But those from certain populations showed great variation in height under culture, some individuals becoming as large as those from normal inland populations. Clearly these populations must have contained biotypes differing widely in their genetical growth potentialities, and in the original habitat uniformity must have been imposed upon all by suppressive environmental factors. In these colonies, ecotype had not entirely replaced

*This term was introduced by Clements to denote ecological forms which were purely the product of environmental modification. It appears to be more widely used than Turesson's own equivalent term, *ecophene*.

ecad; in other colonies, all of whose individuals showed genetical dwarfness in the experimental garden, the process of "genotypical response to habitat" had presumably proceeded to its completion.

Whilst it seems probable that ecotypic adaptation mostly results from selection, either directly as supposed by Turesson, or indirectly in some such manner as that indicated by Waddington, the possibility that adaptation may sometimes arise from the direct transmission of acquired properties from parent to offspring cannot be discounted. In flax, it has been shown that morphological differences arising from variation in mineral nutrition may be transmitted through several generations, and in homozygous lines of peas effects arising from abnormal temperature experiences are cumulative from generation to generation. In inbreeding populations of grasses, including some cereals, the temperature and photo-periodic experiences of parents may be reflected in differences in growth rate and earliness of progeny even when these are grown in uniform neutral environments. Some of these effects are undoubtedly short-term, and probably attributable to physiological effects upon the cytoplasm of the egg, or upon the embryo during its early growth, rather than to changes in the nuclear component of inheritance. Even so, such mechanisms of short-term adaptation may be important in the ecological success of plant populations.

These considerations indicate that it is not permissible to conclude from transplant experiments or even from cultures from seed that an example of apparent ecotypic differentiation is *necessarily* gene-determined; strictly, this can only be established by crossing experiments.

Genecological Research outside of Sweden

The methods of study of the ecological responses of species pioneered by Turesson—the techniques of genecology—were quickly taken up by workers in other countries. Probably the most elaborate of subsequent investigations has been that carried out in California by Clausen, Keck and Hiesey under the auspices of the Carnegie Institute. These workers have studied ecotypical differentiation in several elements of the native flora of California. They have adopted the method of comparative culture in standard environments, and have combined with it studies of the responses of plants in diverse environments along a transect extending from Stanford, at an altitude of 100 ft. near the Pacific coast, through Mather at an altitude of 4,600 ft. in the foothills of the Sierra Nevada, to Timberline, in a valley at 10,000 ft. near the Sierran crest adjoining the eastern boundary of the Yosemite National Park.

From the many species which have been studied genecologically by the Carnegie Institute team, the rosaceous species *Potentilla glandulosa* may be taken as illustrating many principles of general applicability. This species occupies a wide ecological, as well as geographical, range in California, extending from near sea-level to altitudes over 10,000 ft. in the Sierra Nevada. Within this area, investigation showed that four major ecotypes existed and two minor ones. Of the regional ecotypes, one occupied the area of the Californian Coast Range, one was peculiar to the Sierran foothills, another was of the nature of a sub-alpine ecotype in the Sierra Nevada, and the last was high alpine. The ecotypes differed from each other in various morphological features: stature, habit, inflorescence form, leaf size and texture, and petal size, shape and colour. Perhaps more important, they showed dissimilarities in physiological features clearly connected with their capacity for survival in the areas where they occurred naturally, in particular in their seasonal rhythms of growth, flowering and seed ripening, and in their resistance to cold. Hybridisations carried out between representative plants from the various ecotypes suggested that the differences between them, including the physiological ones, were governed by polygenic systems.

The ecotypes defined by Clausen, Keck and Hiesey within *Potentilla glandulosa* (and other species) were often geographically much more extensive than those recognised by Turesson and were themselves genetically heterogeneous. Local populations showed the type of internal variation characteristic of outbreeding species, but between populations classed within the same ecotype, differences were found in stature and other characteristics which could be associated with minor habitat variations.

In the varied-environment transplant experiments, plants from the different ecotypes were cloned, and ramets were grown at the different stations along the altitudinal transect. The outstanding result was to reveal that each possessed different capacities for response, both physiological and morphological, and that in most cases their individualities were retained at the different stations. In general, morphological changes induced were slight in comparison with the far-reaching changes in annual cycles of development which plants of the various ecotypes underwent when taken outside of their natural ranges. Even so, the possible extent of modification of the developmental cycle was not great enough to ensure indefinite survival far outside of the natural range. Thus the Coast Range ecotype of *Potentilla glandulosa* rarely persisted more than a single season at the alpine station at Timberline, where it proved unable to adjust its developmental cycle, timed to the long growing season of coastal California, to the shorter period available for growth. On the other hand, the alpine and sub-alpine ecotypes survived at all transplant stations, although the former showed by its poor growth that it was ill-adapted to the conditions at the low-level station at Stanford. Curiously, both of these ecotypes showed best growth, as judged by vigour and size, at the station of intermediate altitude at Mather. At Timberline, grown side by side, they showed strong superficial resemblance so that had this transfer been the only one made, it might have been concluded that the sub-alpine form could be transformed directly into the alpine one by environmental influences. But the reactions of the two at the other stations were different enough to make clear that they were distinct entities.

In some of the plants investigated by Clausen, Keck and Hiesey, ecological adaptation of races had been accompanied by the appearance of chromosomal differences, with special consequences which are discussed at greater length in a later chapter. But often, as in the case of *Potentilla glandulosa*, the differences between ecotypes were on a "genic" level, and of a quantitative nature of the sort associated with polygenic control. As had Turesson, the Carnegie Institute team interpreted the ecotypes as representing clusters of biotypes selected from the general species population because of their special fitness for particular habitats. Also following Turesson, they emphasised, initially at least, the distinctness of the ecotypes within a species from each other. In *Hieracium umbellatum*, Turesson contended that when dune and inland ecotypes met, there was no smooth intergradation of one into another, but a zone of ecological maladjustment in which occurred hybrids and segregates. Similarly in *Potentilla glandulosa*, Clausen, Keck and Hiesey stated that where two ecotypes met, they produced hybrids which in later generations gave rise to forms variously recombining the parental characters. Other workers have failed to find evidence of such clear cut differentiation of ecotypes and have accordingly introduced modifications of the original concept.

J. W. Gregor and his collaborators, working at the Scottish Plant Breeding Station near Edinburgh, have made an elaborate study of the genecology of the sea plantain, *Plantago maritima*. Large samples from sea plantain colonies in various parts of the northern hemisphere have been grown from seed in standard environments, and statistical studies have been conducted on their expression of several morphological features and on their physiological behaviour. Gregor has emphasised that the distributional pattern of a species like *Plantago maritima* comprises numerous more or less isolated breeding colonies (*gamodemes*) of varying size. Some of these are so small that their structure may be the outcome of random genetical drift, of the sort mentioned in the footnote on p. 39:

the so-called Sewall Wright effect. However, in those in
which the breeding strength was to be numbered in thousands
of individuals, it was concluded that the structure was much
more likely to be the outcome of selective influences of the type
considered to be responsible for the differentiation of ecotypes,
and in collecting samples for the investigation of such differentiation, concentration was upon gamodemes comprising
more than one thousand breeding individuals. One important
outcome of Gregor's work on such units was to reveal that
while certain ecotypes may be separated from each other by
variational discontinuity (as had been considered to be general
by Turesson and Clausen, Keck and Hiesey) more often
ecotypic differentiation is continuous. Thus in the case of
the sea plantains, a clear ecological gradient can very often
be detected in their coastal habitats from the water-logged
mud at lower levels, through salt-marsh to drained coastal
mud. Samples from populations occupying habitats at various
levels in this ecological gradient were grown under standard
conditions, and it was found that for characters such as
scape length and growth habit there was continuous gradation
from the lowest to the highest levels. This is illustrated in
the graphs reproduced in Fig. 5. The concept of discontinuous
ecotypes occupying clearly differentiated habitats cannot
easily be applied to such an example, and Gregor therefore
brought forward the term *ecocline** to denote a situation in
which a species shows genetically based continuously graded
variation which can be correlated with an observable gradient
in environmental conditions. In accordance with the implications of this new concept, the ecotype became redefined
by Gregor as "a particular range on an ecocline." Ecotypes
were presumed to show distinctness only where the habitats
in which they are differentiated are clearly demarcated;
where across a given part of a species range there is constant

*The concept of *clines* was introduced by J. S. Huxley in 1939.
The word may be applied to any situation where, within a single
continuous population, or between neighbouring populations, there is
continuous, fairly evenly graded variation in some morphological
character or characters.

change of one or several environmental factors, the species
may be capable of continuous genotypical adjustment from

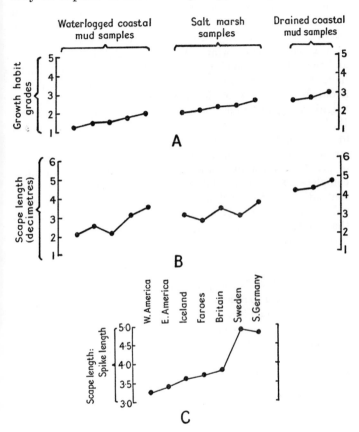

FIG. 5. Ecoclines and topoclines.
    A. Ecocline in growth habit (this is estimated in arbitrary grades
        from 1 to 5).
    B. Ecocline in scape (flowering stalk) length.
    C. Topocline in North Atlantic region in the ratio scape (flowering
        stalk) length: spike (inflorescence) length.
                           All after J. W. Gregor.

colony to colony. The two situations are contrasted in Fig. 6.

Just how close such adaptative adjustment can become in a particular colony will obviously depend mainly upon two factors: the availability of suitable genetical variants in the area concerned from which the new population can be built, and the extent to which the new genetical patterns, once they have been constructed, can retain their individuality and avoid being swamped by continuous cross-breeding with neighbouring individuals not occupying the specialised habitat. Both factors are closely bound up with the degree of isolation of the population. Complete isolation from others of the species would condemn it to reliance upon its own resources of genetical variability which might be inadequate to allow complete adjustment, while insufficient isolation would mean that adjustment of each generation would have to take place independently, since gene exchange with biotypes outside of the habitat would break up the favourable genotypes each breeding cycle.

Taxonomic Problems of Ecotypic Variation

The examples of ecologically variable species quoted above serve to throw into relief some of the taxonomic problems arising from such variability. The morphological differences which are encountered between ecologically differentiated populations tend always to be quantitative rather than qualitative, i.e., to be revealed in the degree to which characters are expressed rather than in the actual presence or absence of distinctive features. They range from those differences which are so minor that they can only be detected by statistical tests, to those which can readily be detected without elaborate measurement. Furthermore, we may have a situation in which extremes of a series of populations are very different from each other although the variational gap between them is completely spanned by a chain of intermediates.

Obviously, regional ecotypes can be fitted into a fairly orthodox scheme of infra-specific categories where they are

clearly demarcated morphologically and geographically.
In the case of *Potentilla glandulosa*, most of the regiona

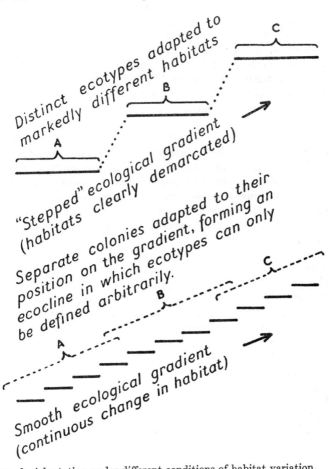

Fig. 6. Adaptation under different conditions of habitat variation.
A. Abrupt habitat change, producing "stepped" ecological gradient.
B. Steady habitat change, producing smooth ecological gradient.
   See text.

5

ecotypes distinguished by Clausen, Keck and Hiesey had already been recognised taxonomically as subspecies. Thus the Coast Range ecotype corresponded to the subsp. *typica*, the foot-hill ecotype to subsp. *reflexa* while the subalpine and alpine ecotypes both belonged to the subsp. *nevadensis*. Similarly, several of the ecotypes recognised by Turesson corresponded to previously named infra-specific groups, ranked variously as "forms," "varieties" and "subspecies." Turesson's observations suggested that parallel ecotypes were differentiated in different species in similar habitat conditions, and he therefore suggested that unity of treatment could be introduced by naming the ecotypes in each according to the habitats in which they occurred. The ecotype of *Hieracium umbellatum* found in shifting dunes, corresponding in part to f. *filifolium*, thus became *H. umbellatum* oecotypus *arenarius*; the maritime ecotype of the red campion, *Melandrium rubrum*, corresponding to var. *crassifolium*, became *M. rubrum* oecotypus *salinus*, and so forth.

Naturally such treatment as these, being no more than extensions of the classical taxonomic method, depend upon the possibility of clear recognition of distinct habitat-types. Where integradation of forms is encountered, the "type" treatment becomes impossible, or only possible at the expense of purely arbitrary division of the observed variation range. For some such situations, Gregor has indicated the possibility of taxonomic treatment by defining ecoclines. But even this does not cover all the variation found within a species like *P. maritima*, where superimposed on ecological variation there is regional variation which is not directly associable with particular habitat conditions, a type considered in the following chapter.

CHAPTER V

GEOGRAPHICAL VARIATION
AND REPRODUCTIVE ISOLATION

THE basis for the recognition of ecotypes within a species is simply that the occurrence of populations with certain heritable adaptative characteristics in common should be correlatable with particular conditions of habitat. Although much infraspecific variation is of this nature, it is commonly found that populations from different areas differ morphologically even when no obvious differences in their habitats exist. Furthermore, it is often the case that over and above the local ecological variation there is regional variation which can hardly be looked upon as directly adaptative.

Non-Adaptative Population Differentiation

As we have seen, in small populations it is possible that random genetical drift may lead to the fixation of particular genes and loss of others even without (or against) the pressure of natural selection. Highly anomalous minor populations of plants often occur on remote islands and isolated mountain summits, and it is probable that many owe their distinctive characters to this process. Examples are to be found in the mountain flora of the British Isles, in which there are several species which appear to be relicts from the time when sub-arctic conditions prevailed over most of the country during the final phase of the last Ice Age. During the period of climatic improvement which followed the final retreat of the ice, these species were eliminated in the lowland districts (where, however, sub-fossil remains of some of them have been found) and persisted only in small colonies in widely scattered (and thus genetically isolated) stations in the mountain districts. It is often the case that these small isolated populations show little internal variability and differ from each other in constant characteristics, from which we may deduce that in each locality a different small group of biotypes has survived. A typical example is that of the alpine rock-cress, *Arabis petraea*, which is often found to differ quite markedly, even from mountain to mountain in the same district, in such features as leaf shape and size, the differences being maintained in cultivation. Since it is usually not possible to detect differential environmental factors which might have caused the striking morphological divergence between isolated colonies of plants like *Arabis petraea*, and furthermore since the same species often occur through much wider ranges of habitats in their continental areas without showing such marked local differentiation, it seems likely that the character-istic facies of each micro-population has arisen through random fixation of particular, not necessarily adaptative, gene patterns. However, the possibility still remains that selective biotype elimination may have taken place in the past under the influence of differential climatic factors not now discernible, perhaps during the period of the post-glacial climatic optimum, when the climate of the British Isles is known to have been warmer than today or any other time since the final disappear-ance of the ice, and when conditions must have been at their worst for the late-glacial survivors.

In species not possessing relict distributions, differences between small local populations which cannot be readily explained ecologically are often found to be present. At least some of this variability can be ascribed to chance, where the genetical constitution of a colony of a species occupying a particular habitat has depended upon the geno-type of the first seed (or small group of seeds) which has happened to arrive in the area. The total genetical varia-bility of the colony will depend initially upon the heterozy-gosity of the first colonist or colonists, and the biotypes of which it consists must necessarily be grouped closely around the originals until mutation or further immigration enriches the store of genetical variability. Water-plants appear to provide good examples of the operation of this principle. The common white water-lily, *Nymphaea alba*, occurs practically throughout the British Isles. Isolated colonies often show great individuality in such features as size of leaves and flowers and numbers of floral parts. Furthermore, different colonies

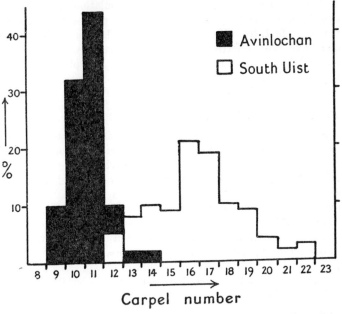

FIG. 7. Variation of carpel number in two different populations of the white water-lily, *Nymphaea alba*, from Avinlochan, Inverness-shire, and the Isle of South Uist. There is a considerable difference in the intrinsic variability of the two populations as well as in the mean carpel number.

vary widely in the amount of *internal* variation which they show, some containing a very narrow range of biotypes and others very wide. The histograms reproduced in Fig. 7 illustrate the variation in number of carpels in flowers from fifty plants selected at random from two colonies: an extremely variable one from the Isle of South Uist, Outer

Hebrides, and a singularly invariable one, from Avinlochan, Inverness-shire. Not only does the total variability differ, but the average number of carpels is different in the two populations. Since this character, carpel-number, is closely correlated with others such as number of stamens, number and size of petals, and leaf size, the populations from these two localities look quite different from each other. As a matter of fact, from time to time colonies like the Avinlochan one have been referred to a different "species," *Nymphaea occidentalis*. Since the variation ranges overlap, of course, bio-types could be selected from the South Uist population which would be quite identical with those occurring in Avinlochan.

Types of Regional Variation

So far, our discussion of infraspecific variation has centred around the local population, and we have seen some of the ways in which differences between such populations can arise—through the influence of selective factors bringing about ecotypic differentiation, through random genetical drift, and through genetical differences between the individuals which happen to have originated isolated colonies. Generally speaking, a species distribution takes the form of a mosaic of local populations of greater or less degree of isolation, and therefore it is to be expected that most will show a degree of microgeographical variation, part of it correlatable with differences in habitat, and part apparently fortuitous. However, on a higher level than the local population, *regional* variation within a species is a very frequent phenomenon, and it is in fact this form of infraspecific variation which has received most taxonomic attention.

In general, taxonomists have hesitated to describe and classify single aberrant populations of a purely local nature, but have been prepared to give recognition to the situation found in many species where, throughout an appreciable segment of their range, the form which happens initially to have been taken as "typical" is replaced by another differing in one or several morphological features.

Such situations have been given great prominence in zoological taxonomy, presumably mainly because in motile animals capable of voluntarily selecting their habitats in different regions, this form of regional race differentiation is usually more obvious than the often more local differentiation which is characteristic of plants. In bird taxonomy in particular the concept of the polytypic species (or *Rassenkreis* —literally "circle of races") has been developed, but it has also found wide application in all of those animal groups in which sufficient descriptive work has been done to reveal the true pattern of geographical variation, replacing in these groups the more static Linnæan species concept. In zoological practice, the geographical subdivisions of species are given trinomials. The red grouse, *Lagopus scoticus*, for example, exists with us in two subspecies, *Lagopus scoticus scoticus*, representing the populations in Scotland, northern England and Wales, and *Lagopus scoticus hibernicus*, the Irish populations.

The type of situation which admirably fits the Rassenkreis-concept can be represented diagrammatically as in Fig. 8A. Clear variational discontinuities exist between the aggregate populations of the various sectors, so that any individual from any sector can be placed immediately on its morphological attributes alone. *Within* each region, there may be a degree of variation between local populations, ecotypical or otherwise. If the attributes affected are not those involved in the regional variation, or if the range of variation within regions does not span the gap between them, the situation is not basically changed, but can be represented as in Fig. 8B. Individuals can still be placed purely on the basis of their morphological attributes. Generally, a pattern of a clear-cut nature like this, with races abruptly replacing each other geographically (and thus said to be *vicarious*) is only encountered where discontinuities are imposed by geographical features—mountain ranges, seas and the like. In botanical taxonomic practice the biological significance of this type of distributional pattern has rarely been taken seriously into account, and generally speaking the taxonomic ranks ascribed to the isolated sectors have been

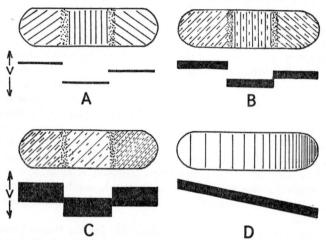

FIG. 8. Types of geographical variation. In each figure, the ellipse represents the total distributional area, which is broken into three segments by topographical barriers (marked by dotted bands) in A, B and C but not in D. The range of morphological variation is shown at V, the thickness of the rectangles indicating the range of internal variability in the population "segment" immediately above.

    A. The three population segments are morphologically quite distinct, and the internal variability of each is small. In taxonomic practice, each would probably receive recognition as "species."

    B. The internal variability of each population segment is greater, but there is no overlapping, and every individual from each segment could be identified correctly without knowledge of its origin. The segments would be recognised as "species" or possibly "subspecies."

    C. The internal variability of each population segment is high, and all three overlap, so that they can be discriminated only statistically; certain individuals could not be placed on the basis of morphology alone. The segments would be recognised as "subspecies."

    D. No topographical barriers are present, and there is a continuous character-gradient or cline. If this were unknown, individuals or even colonies from different parts of the area might be considered to differ sufficiently to be named as "species."

based simply upon their degree of morphological dissimilarity. If this has been large (and particularly, although it is quite irrelevant biologically, where the isolating physical barrier has been appreciable, like the Atlantic Ocean) they have been ranked as separate species; if small, as subspecies. Examples are manifold, but perhaps the best group of cases is to be found in the floras of the two sides of the North Atlantic, in which innumerable species-pairs can be pointed out, one

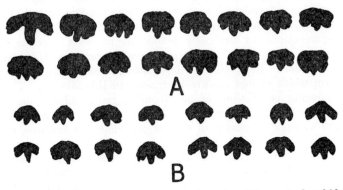

FIG. 9. Flower variation range in two subspecies of the spotted orchid, *Orchis fuchsii*.
A. subsp. *hebridensis*, from the Isle of South Uist; and,
B. subsp. *fuchsii* from Hampshire.
In each case a random sample of 16 plants has been taken from a colony of the subspecies, and a corresponding flower removed from the inflorescence of each. What are shown in the figure are silhouettes of the largest petals ("labella") from each one of these flowers.

member of each pair often filling an ecological niche on one side of the Atlantic identical with that filled by the other member on the other side. Thus European wood sorrel, *Oxalis acetosella*, is represented in eastern North America by *O. montana*; the yellow water-lily, *Nuphar luteum*, by *N. americanum*; may-lily, *Maianthemum bifolium*, by *M. canadense*; way-faring tree, *Viburnum lantana* by *V. alnifolium* and so on. The actual morphological differences which have served as bases for the recognition as separate species of related populations on the two sides of the Atlantic have often been quite minor: thus the qualitative feature consistently differentiating the American mountain ash, *Sorbus americana*, from the European, *S. aucuparia*, is merely the hairless, sticky winter buds of the former contrasted with the hairy, dark-brown buds of the latter.

Notwithstanding any disagreement there may be as to the taxonomic ranks to be given to the divergent sectors in variation patterns such as those represented in Figs 8A and 8B, the significant feature is that these patterns *do* lend themselves to treatment by orthodox taxonomic methods dependent on the recognition of morphological differences between individuals. Regional race differentiation frequently is of a form which cannot readily be treated in this manner. The aggregate populations of neighbouring geographical regions may be found to differ from each other only in small shifts in the average expression of certain morphological features, or perhaps only in the proportional representation of certain distinctive biotypes. The characters affected might be just those which *within* regions concerned show variation between local populations, so that local and regional variation are superimposed. The pattern is then of the type represented in Fig. 8c. Situations of this nature can be investigated only by statistical methods, but when the pattern has been revealed, there remains still some possibility of fitting it into the orthodox system of taxonomic nomenclature.

As illustrative examples, two species of spotted orchid occurring in north-western Europe may be taken. In the British Isles the common spotted orchid, *Orchis fuchsii*, is replaced in some islands of the Hebrides and in parts of western Ireland by a subspecies, subsp. *hebridensis*.* The

---

*According to the International Code of Botanical Nomenclature (see p. 112), when the first subspecies is named under a species which has not previously been split up, another subspecies is formed which contains the original "type" of the species. The naming of *O. fuchsii* subsp. *hebridensis* meant, therefore, that the common southern English race became *O. fuchsii* subsp. *fuchsii*.

variation ranges of the two overlap, so that identical biotypes occur in the two distributional areas, and these could not be referred to one or the other subspecies on morphological grounds alone: knowledge of the place of origin would be necessary. The flower variation ranges of the two subspecies are illustrated in Fig. 9: the overlapping character is clear, but so is the fact that the populations as wholes are different. In another species of spotted orchid, *Orchis maculata*, the British population in the aggregate differs in certain floral features from that occurring in eastern Sweden, where Linnæus collected the specimen which is the nomenclatural "type" of the species, i.e. the plant to which the name *O. maculata* was first applied. The British population has been distinguished as the subspecies *ericetorum*, that in the Swedish lowlands thus becoming *O. maculata* subsp. *maculata*. It is interesting to note that in this species an ecological distinction exists between the two subspecies, the British one occurring characteristically in rather open habitats on acid, peaty soils, whilst the subsp. *maculata* is more a plant of woodlands.

Continuous Geographical Variation

Presumably the patterns of Figs. 8A, B and C all represent the results of the one process: genetical drift apart of segments of a formerly continuous species-population after their isolation from each other by geographical barriers. Race differentiation can, however, proceed without the intervention of major barriers, through progressive smooth shifts of average character expression from local population to local population. This is the type of situation illustrated in Fig. 8D. In a species with an extensive range, small amounts of gene-exchange may be possible between neighbouring panmictic populations, but between the extremes the *actual* rate of gene-exchange achieved may be so slight as to be negligible, even although no actual distributional breaks occur in between. Spatial separation may thus itself be an isolating factor, and a fair degree of genetical divergence between remote populations may be possible. This is likely to lead to phenotypical gradients of the type illustrated in Fig. 8D; gradients which are termed *clines* (see footnote on p. 54). Across a continent, or over a series of latitudinal climatic belts, such variation may actually be ecologically conditioned, and so ecoclinal in Gregor's sense, being the product of what is in effect a selection gradient. Or it may be non-adaptative, the product perhaps of historical factors, a form which Gregor has denoted as a *topocline*. An example of a topocline detected by Gregor in the sea-plantain, in the ratio scape-length to spike-length, is illustrated in Fig. 5c.

Clinal variation, by its very nature, is untreatable by taxonomic methods which demand the recognition of "types." Even where a cline involves correlated change in several morphological characters, no system of categories such as "species," "subspecies" and "variety" can give adequate expression to the actual form of the variation. When, as has been demonstrated in some cases, independent topoclines exist for different morphological features which do not run parallel, or where ecoclines or topoclines intersect, the "type" method is totally defeated. Specification of the clines in terms of the affected characters and the geographical areas across which they vary is then the only possibility if it is desired to give expression to the existing variation. It may, of course, be necessary to refer to a particular regional population within a cline, and for this purpose Gregor has proposed the term *topotype*, which he defines as a population in a geographical region possessing characters differing from those of another region. A topotype is *intraclinal* when it refers to a particular range in a topocline (note that this definition is parallel to the redefinition proposed by Gregor for the ecotype); and *extraclinal* when the regional population concerned cannot be fitted into a cline. Locally differentiated minor populations occupying like habitats are termed *microtopotypes* in this system.

Reproductive Isolation

For a genetically differentiated population of an outbreeding plant to maintain its identity over a period of time, one of two conditions must prevail: either the pressure of environmental selection must be such as to overcome the levelling-out effect of cross-pollination from other populations and so to maintain a similar biotype composition from generation to generation, or the population must be insulated against the effects of crossing by some form of reproductive isolation.

In a species like *Plantago maritima* which shows ecotypical differentiation on a very local scale, it may well be that colonies occupying extreme habitats retain similar facies from generation to generation in spite of pollination from outside sources through the continuous differential elimination of biotypes. However, in general, the genetical divergence of different populations of a species is always likely to be favoured by some degree of reproductive isolation.

In our discussion of infraspecific variation so far, we have been mainly concerned with situations in which reproductive isolation has been imposed simply by the geographical or microgeographical separation of the divergent populations. We have, in fact, tacitly adopted a postulate about the structure of amphimictic species, namely, that the populations of which they are composed, whether or not they differ genetically, remain potentially capable of interbreeding. Turesson in his early writings, wishing to direct attention to the ecological aspect of the species problem, coined the term *ecospecies* to denote " . . . the Linnæan species or genotype compounds as they are realised in nature," the ecotypes being contained within the ecospecies, and representing themselves the products ". . . arising as a result of the genotypical response of an ecospecies to a particular habitat." This defines what might be termed the positive aspect: what an ecospecies is presumed to contain. In his later writings, Turesson found the need for defining also the negative aspect of ecospecies, namely, what they do *not* contain. To do this he was impelled to introduce a new criterion which was genetical rather than ecological in nature: that of intersterility. His definition of the ecospecies given in 1929 is as follows: "An amphimict-population the constituents of which in nature produce vital and fertile descendants with each other giving rise to less vital or more or less sterile descendants in nature, however, when crossed with constituents of any other population."

Turesson was by no means the first to introduce the sterility-fertility criterion of species: as we have seen on p. 4 something of the sort was implied in John Lindley's definition of 1837, and particularly among zoologists the idea of intersterility as a test of specific distinction has long been popular. In plant taxonomy, the importance of Turesson's introduction of the criterion lay mainly in the relationships of the ecospecies with the other categories of variation which he proposed. We shall have occasion to discuss these in greater detail in a later chapter. Here we must devote some attention to the types of factors which bring about the reproductive isolation of populations of plants, since this is a matter of the greatest importance to taxonomy, playing as it does a leading part in the formation and maintenance of the pattern of natural variation with which taxonomy has to deal.

At the expense of a certain degree of over-simplification, it is possible to classify isolating mechanisms into three general groups:

(a) those which operate outside of the plant, tending to prevent cross-pollination between groups;

(b) those which operate inside of the plant tending to prevent fertilisation, or to bring about the failure of the hybrid zygote to develop before it commences independent life, and

(c) those which take effect in the hybrid progeny, tending to reduce its viability and chances of reaching reproductive maturity in nature, or to reduce or destroy its fertility.

(a) *External factors*

The most obvious factor tending to prevent the inter-breeding of two populations is spatial separation, which may, of course, be imposed by different habitat preferences and thus be a form of ecological isolation. The effectiveness of geographical separation in preventing interbreeding is governed primarily by the pollination mechanisms of the plants concerned. Collections made in the upper atmosphere have shown that the pollen of forest trees, grasses and other wind-pollinated species are carried by air movements to great altitudes, and data on pollen-rain in built-up areas, ships at sea and the like, reveal that very considerable horizontal transport is achieved as a result. A gap of a few miles between populations, say of pines or oaks, may therefore be of minor significance. In the case of plants like these, the effective amount of interbreeding between populations will depend upon the proportions of local and foreign pollen in the atmosphere at each station during the flowering period: naturally the amount of foreign pollen will become lower as the distance of a population from others increases, but *complete* reproductive isolation will be the lot only of those which are extremely remote.

In contrast, isolation of populations of insect-pollinated species may be total in the space of a few hundred yards, for it is often the case that pollinating insects are themselves strongly limited ecologically, visiting only those plants growing within their chosen habitat. Where such ecological specialisation of pollen-vectors is found, conditions are ideal for the maintenance of the integrity of ecologically differentiated plant populations.

Several factors are known which may act to restrict the crossing of related species occupying the same area. Lack of coincidence of flowering periods is effective both in wind- and insect-pollinated species. Isolation of this type may be seasonal, where flowering takes place at different times of year, or the flowering seasons may overlap but the pollen may be shed at different times of day. An interesting case of the latter has recently been investigated in the bent-grass genus, *Agrostis*. The two species, *A. tenuis* and *A. canina*, are prevented from interbreeding in nature largely because the pollen of the former is commonly shed in the morning and that of the latter in the evening, and since the stigmas of the respective species are only receptive at the appropriate time of day, cross-pollination is not frequent.

Extreme flower-specificity on the part of pollen-vectors is apparently a rather frequent cause for the failure of cross-pollination of related species growing together. Particular colours, scents and shapes of flowers may exert special attraction for specific insects, which may in their pollinating movements visit only those flowers which match their special preference. The effect of such "assortative" pollination, as it is termed, is to bring about the fertilisation of like by like, so tending to maintain the integrity of the particular gene pattern which produces the phenotype attractive to the insect. An interesting example is provided by the orchidaceous genus, *Ophrys*, in the Mediterranean region. In this genus, the flowers often bear a striking resemblance to various insects, as can be seen in two British representatives, the bee orchid, *O. apifera*, and the fly orchid, *O. muscifera*. In southern Europe and North Africa, where several *Ophrys* species occur together, the flowers of the different species bear a resemblance to the females of different hymenopterous insects. Pollination is brought about through the agency of the males of these insects, which are deceived by the resemblance and alight on the flowers. Since each insect is attracted by only one pattern of flower, pollination is necessarily assortative, and hybrids between the different *Ophrys* species are rarely produced.

Mechanical specialisation of the pollination apparatus is another means by which pollination of like by like is ensured. As in many orchids, it may take the form of mechanical adaptation of flowers so that the pollination mechanism can be operated only by specific insects, which are in turn specific in their selection of flowers to visit. In some instances, as in the milk-weed family, *Asclepiadaceae*, the pollen is presented to visiting insects in solid masses (pollinia) rather than in a loose powder, and for successful pollination these have to be inserted into appropriately shaped slits on the style—a form of "lock and key" mechanism.

(b) *Internal Factors*

Should cross-pollination of different species occur, several factors may intervene to prevent the production of viable hybrid progeny. The most generally effective is the simple fact that unless a degree of relationship exists between the species, the foreign pollen does not germinate on the stigma, or if it does, the foreign pollen-tubes grow so slowly through the style that they cannot compete with those of the same species should they also be present. It is only necessary to look at the stigma of a female oak flower in spring to realise that it is capable of collecting pollen of many other genera than its own, but that these foreign pollen grains interfere in no way with the breeding of the oak, simply because they do not germinate or are killed shortly after germination.

(c) *Factors in Hybrid Progeny*

Presuming that fertilisation is achieved, successful development of the embryo demands that harmony should exist between the parental chromosome sets, and between the zygote nucleus and the cytoplasm surrounding it which is derived from the female parent. Disharmony between genomes may express itself at any stage from fertilisation onwards, and may result in total developmental failure or in weakly abnormal growth. Even if viability is not impaired directly, hybrid genotypes may prove to be ecologically ill-adapted and incapable of competing with parental stocks in nature. Although complete interfertility may exist, two species may grow side by side for long periods without losing their identities simply through the rapid elimination of hybrid progeny which fall between the centres of variation represented by the two parents. In the oak genus, *Quercus*, in

6

North America, species which grow together without inter-grading despite their interfertility, and are known from the fossil record to have done so for protracted periods, may owe their continued independence to this type of isolation.

Even presuming that first generation hybrids reach maturity, their existence cannot prejudice the continued independence of the parental groups unless they possess a degree of inter-fertility allowing them to breed amongst themselves, or to back-cross with parental stocks. Causes of hybrid infertility may be grouped into two classes: those associated with gene and chromosome irregularities respectively.

The course of sporogenesis, involving the meiotic nuclear division, is, of course, itself subject to control by the genotype of the plant, and genotypic disharmony in hybrids may strike at this process as at any other in the life of the individual. Should sporogenesis be successfully carried through, the haploid generation—brief although it is in flowering-plants—provides a further test for the fitness of the nuclei produced by meiosis. An ill-co-ordinated haploid genome resulting from the segregation of incompatible parental contributions may prevent the production of normal embryo-sacs or male gametophytes, without cytological irregularities being actually visible.

Incompatibility of parental genomes expressed in differences in numbers of chromosomes, or in differences of their gross structure, is a frequent (and cytologically readily detectable) source of hybrid sterility. In plants, species often differ from each other in their numbers of chromosomes, and chromosome numbers in groups of related species are commonly found to form an arithmetic progression, based upon the lowest number present in the group. This is the phenomenon of polyploidy, discussed at greater length in the next chapter. In hybrids between species possessing dissimilar chromosome numbers, complete pairing of the parental chromosome sets at the time of the meiotic division is not usually possible. Either some chromosomes are left unpaired, or groups of three or more are produced. In any case, grave irregularity in the meiotic division usually ensues, and generally the majority of the resultant nuclei are so seriously unbalanced in their chromosome complements as to be inviable, leading to partial or complete sterility.

Even without a difference in chromosome number, the structure of the chromosomes of two related species may be unlike through the different arrangement in them of whole blocks of genes. In hybrids between species which differ in this manner, the pairing process of early meiosis may be upset through the attempts of corresponding gene-blocks to pair even when they occur in segments of different, mainly non-homologous, chromosomes. This commonly leads to the formation of complicated groups of three or more partly matched chromosomes, and so to irregularities in the distribution of genes to the daughter nuclei which accordingly show some degree of inviability (see page 89).

The causes of reproductive isolation discussed above do not operate with complete independence in nature. In any particular situation, it is usually the case that several factors reinforce one another. The two spotted orchid species, *Orchis maculata* and *O. fuchsii*, mentioned earlier, provide an example of this. In Britain, *O. maculata* subsp. *ericetorum* and *O. fuchsii* do not usually grow together because of their different ecological tolerances, the former preferring acid soils and the latter those which are base-rich. But even where they occur together, there is little possibility of complete intergradation of the two leading to loss of their independence as species because they possess different chromosome numbers, *O. fuchsii* with the diploid number of 40, and the subsp. *ericetorum* with 80 (Fig. 10). The hybrid, with 60, is highly sterile due to meiotic irregularities which lead to the distribution of irregular chromosome numbers to the spore nuclei.

The Breakdown of Isolation

Hybridisation in nature between populations normally isolated reproductively from each other is a frequent source of variational anomaly. For it to take place, the bars to crossing which normally act to keep the populations apart must in some way be overcome. Of those discussed above, the most easily surmounted are those which operate to prevent cross-pollination, particularly those dependent on spatial separation. Reproductive contacts can be established between populations, previously isolated geographically, through the migration of one into the area of the other, and even strong ecological specialisation may be inadequate to prevent cross-breeding when two species invade dissimilar habitats which are closely juxtaposed, or neutral habitats suitable for both. In the last phase of the earth's history, human activities such as felling, draining and burning have upset many natural ecological barriers, and in species where internal bars to crossing have not been present, have provided the opportunity for hybridisation, sometimes on a vast scale.

The results of hybridisation must be considered on two levels: the *immediate*, observable within a short period after the reproductive contact has been made, and the *long-term*, developing as a permanent alteration to the previous variation pattern. The short-term effect commonly produced by the free interbreeding of previously isolated groups is often quite spectacular. Whereas the first hybrid generation tends to be intermediate between the parents, particularly in those characters which are governed polygenically, in the second generation, segregation and recombination of the parental gene-complexes take place. The result is often a bizarre collection of individuals recombining in various degrees the differentiating characters of the parents. Such a group is known as a *hybrid-swarm*. Where the parents are known from other parts of their ranges in a "pure" form, such swarms are easily enough interpreted, and if their genesis is sufficiently clear, taxonomic difficulties do not arise unless excessively enthusiastic name-coiners are tempted to describe and christen the various segregates. But in little-known floras, particularly where conditions for hybrid-swarm formation have arisen only recently through human occupation, their presence may add greatly to the difficulties of taxonomists. A flora in which very many different genera contain species-complexes which are confused by hybrid-swarm formation is that of New Zealand, where the advent of the white man has no doubt upset many ecological barriers in comparatively recent times. It is also possible that part of the present remarkable amount of natural hybridisation in the floras of both Australia and New Zealand may be due to the reduction in efficiency of barriers to cross-pollination following the introduction of that highly active pollinator, the hive-bee.

The formation of hybrid-swarms may itself be no more than an evanescent phenomenon, but there appear to be several ways in which natural hybridisation can produce a long-term effect upon the variation pattern of a group. Theoretically, at least, reproductive contact between two formerly isolated species, maintained over a long enough period of time, could lead to complete breakdown of their individual gene patterns and to the fusion of what were originally two variational foci into one. Although there are no documented cases of the total loss of species by this process, many examples are available of the complete submergence of small populations of one species by a numerically superior relative in the same district. Marsden-Jones and Turrill have investigated cases of this nature in the knapweed genus, *Centaurea*. In Britain, the species *C. nigra* is widespread, while *C. jacea* is usually local. Hybridisation takes place wherever the two come into contact, usually with the production at first of complex hybrid-swarms. Where the *C. jacea* population has been a small and isolated one, the outcome has usually been that it has disappeared in pure form as a result of constant out-breeding, leaving its mark only in enhanced variability of the *C. nigra* populations of the neighbourhood. Pure populations of the two species exist elsewhere in Europe, and the local occurrence of this form of hybridisation does not prejudice their continued existence as separate species.

The example of the Centaureas suggests one method in

which a permanent effect may be registered on a species as a result of hybridisation with others—a method which has recently been subjected to much investigation in America by the geneticist Anderson. Without necessarily leading to the disappearance of specific identities, *occasional* hybridisation may provide a link between two species through which gene-exchange can take place, allowing the genetical variability of one species to be enriched or modified by contributions from the other. The occurrence of gene-leakage from one species into another is termed by Anderson *introgression*, and the process which brings it about, *introgressive hybridisation*. There is now much evidence to suggest that introgression may have an important evolutionary role, especially during periods of flux, when due to geological or other causes the existing ecological order is subject to change. The variational anomalies which introgression produces can be recognised by techniques devised by Anderson for the assessment and study of character correlations in natural populations, for, generally speaking, the effects of introgression are primarily to "pull-out" or polarise the pattern of morphological variation of a species in the direction of the introgressant. From the point of view of the success of the species affected, the mere fact that its store of genetical variation is increased by such a process may add to its ecological potentialities, and therefore be of long-term evolutionary significance. There is a parallel here with the type of situation which, as we saw on p. 56, gives greatest adaptative flexibility within species—partial but not complete isolation of populations so that each can tap the resources of genetical variability of the other, without the occurrence of sufficient interbreeding to prevent some degree of independent differentiation.

CHAPTER VI

CYTOLOGY AND TAXONOMY

DURING the division of a cell, the material of the nucleus condenses into a number of ellipsoidal or rod-shaped bodies which show a high affinity for certain stains and are hence known as chromosomes. The chromosomes of the plant cell have become important to taxonomy in two connections; firstly, since their numbers, sizes and shapes can be used as classificatory criteria like any other morphological features, and secondly, in a more fundamental role, because they sometimes offer direct evidence relating to the nature and origin of variation.

Chromosome Number and Morphology as Taxonomic Characters

The cytological investigation of plants began rather more than half a century ago, and one of its earliest results was to reveal that considerable variation existed in the number and morphology of the chromosomes present in different Linnæan species, and that occasionally differences of the same order occurred *within* Linnæan species, characterising sometimes varieties or subspecies. With improvements in the ease and speed of cytological technique, examination of chromosome complements has become now almost a routine operation in the investigation of critical taxonomic groups. The stage at which the chromosome set is seen at its best is at the metaphase of mitotic division. For taxonomic studies it is customary to prepare sections of root-tips, young leaves or other tissues in which rapid cell division is in progress to obtain nuclei in this state, and to use differential staining techniques to make the chromosomes visible for microscopic study. The appearance of the chromosomes at mitotic metaphase is known as the *karyotype*.

The most easily observable karyotypic differences are those involving chromosome number, particularly the phenomenon of *polyploidy*, mentioned briefly in the last chapter. An example of a polyploid series—one of the longest in the British flora—is provided by the willow genus, *Salix*. In this genus, the base number, i.e., the haploid number of the lowest member, is 19*. Among the species falling at the different levels are: common osier, *S. viminalis*, diploid, $2n=38$; common sallow, *S. atrocinerea*, tetraploid, $2n=76$; tea-leaved willow, *S. phylicifolia*, hexaploid, $2n=114$, and the rare Scottish *S. myrsinites*, octoploid, $2n=152$. It will be noted that in this amphimictic genus, the odd numbers of the polyploid series do not characterise any of the species. It is understandable that this should be so, because the normal pairing procedure of the early phase of meiosis necessitates that each chromosome shall be able to find a homologue, and with an odd number of sets this would be impossible. Triploids, with $2n=57$ have been found in the genus *Salix* as individual plants, but they are highly sterile because of the resultant meiotic irregularities. On the other hand, in apomictic groups the odd members of polyploid series can be perpetuated because reproduction does not involve meiosis. In the mainly apomictic genus *Rubus*, the base number of which is 7, various apomictic biotypes are known with numbers of 14, 21, 28, 35, 42 and 49 in Europe, and higher members of the same series occur in North America. Another homely example is that of the common dandelion, *Taraxacum officinale*. All that have been cytologically examined of the hundred or more forms of this in Britain are apomictic and triploid, with $2n=24$, the base number of the genus being 8. These facts

*In referring to chromosome numbers in polyploid series, a conventional reference system is adopted. The base number of the series is symbolised as x, so that the lowest member of the series would have a somatic number $2x$, a tetraploid, $4x$, a hexaploid, $6x$ and so on. However, in quoting the chromosome number of an individual plant, whether it is in a polyploid series or not, the gametic number is symbolised as n, and the "diploid" (somatic) number as $2n$, even although it may be polyploid with reference to the base number x if the plant happens to belong in a polyploid series.

suggest that chromosome numbers may often give a clue to reproductive irregularities like apomixis, and apomixis has in fact first been detected in some genera through some species being consistently triploid.

When in a polyploid series a plant possesses an exact multiple of the basic chromosome set, it is said to be *euploid*, and where not, *aneuploid*. Aneuploid individuals are occasionally encountered in species which are mostly euploid; as well as often being distinguishable morphologically from others, they naturally also show meiotic irregularities. Sometimes one species in a polyploid series is consistently found to be aneuploid, departing from the expected number by a pair or even two pairs of homologous chromosomes. In some genera, the sequences of chromosome numbers which appear cannot be associated in any particular series, when they are said to be *dysploid*. An example is the sedge genus, *Carex*, in which a very wide range of numbers occurs, ranging from $2n=14$ in the divided sedge, *C. divisa*, to $2n=112$ in the hairy sedge, *C. hirta*. Multiples of 7 are most frequent, but other series may also be present based upon 5, 6 and 8.

Other taxonomically useful characteristics of karyotypes, apart from the matter of chromosome number, are found in the gross morphology of the chromosomes where these are large enough for good microscopical observation. The chromosomes of any one complement often show constant differences in their length at mitotic metaphase, although rarely is there any variability in width. A cardinal feature of each chromosome of the set is the so-called spindle attachment region, usually visible as a marked constriction at some point along its length. Since this position is constant, the chromosomes can be characterised by the relative lengths of their arms. In addition to the primary constriction, there may be others occupying constant positions in particular chromosomes, sometimes so near the ends that they set off small, almost spherical segments known as satellites. Because of these characteristic morphological features, in some very favourable species it is possible to distinguish as individuals every chromosome of the complement. Where this is the case the karyotype can be of considerable taxonomic value, because related species, while possessing chromosomes of the same general type, are often found to show constant differences in their gross morphology. It is sometimes possible to recognise similar chromosomes in the karyotypes of related species and even to detect differences which suggest where segments have been lost or added. Examples of karyotypes of related and unrelated species are illustrated in Fig. 10.

The taxonomic value of cytological data varies from group to group. In some large alliances, it has had practically no significance, either on the species level or above. A family in which this is so is the *Fagaceae*, that to which the oak, beech and chestnut genera belong. The vast majority of chromosome determinations made in this alliance show $2n=24$, and the karyotypes have little or no systematic value. In those alliances in which cytological studies have proved of importance, it is possible to distinguish the special aspect concerned with the inter-relationships of species which is discussed further below, from that affecting the classification of higher units. On the levels of genera, tribes and families, the contribution of karyotypic data has been mainly to suggest affinities or possible lines of division between groups. In the majority of cases, it has actually turned out that data from this source have simply served to justify or reinforce existing classifications based upon morphological criteria. At times, cytological evidence has helped to decide between competing morphological classifications, or to suggest improvements or amendments. Only very rarely has evidence from this source resulted in major taxonomic revisions.

A few examples will help to illustrate the types of karyotypic variation existing in the higher groups. Differences in chromosome number are sometimes found to distinguish units already separated on morphological grounds, while elsewhere there is no such correlation. Particular base numbers may characterise families, sub-families, tribes or genera, in which case a cytological classification would produce lines of demarcation showing some agreement with those based upon morphological criteria. On the other hand, heterogeneous numbers may occur within groups which possess

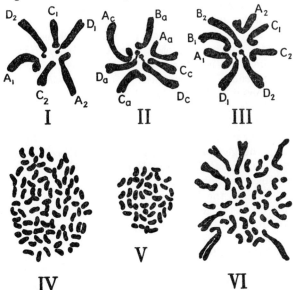

FIG. 10. Somatic chromosomes of flowering-plants, all seen at mitotic metaphase.

   i. *Crepis capillaris,* $2n=6$; homologous chromosomes are lettered alike.

  ii. *Crepis capillaris* X *C. aspersa,* $2n=7$. In the hybrid, the parental chromosome sets can be distinguished, and are denoted by the appropriate suffixes.

 iii. *C. aspersa,* $2n=8$; homologous chromosomes are lettered alike, and to correspond with the plate of *C. capillaris,* which has a similar complement less the pair of "B" chromosomes.

 iv. *Orchis maculata* subsp. *ericetorum,* $2n=80$.

  v. *O. fuchsii,* $2n=40$. In these two spotted orchid species, the chromosomes are small and all of much the same size and shape so that they cannot readily be distinguished from each other.

 vi. *Epipactis atropurpurea,* $2n=40$. In this species, also in the Orchidaceae, there is great variation in the size of the chromosomes in a single complement. It is possible to distinguish homologous pairs among the larger ones, but not among many of the smaller.

obvious morphological unity, and any cytological classification based upon chromosome number has then little or no
meaning.   An order which strikingly illustrates these points
is the *Centrospermae* which, among others, includes the families
Chenopodiaceae (with such familiar plants as beetroot and
spinach) and *Caryophyllaceae* (pinks, campions, catchflys,
stitchworts, chickweeds, etc.).   In the *Chenopodiaceae* the
base chromosome number is 9, and this runs through all the
European genera.   In contrast, in the *Caryophyllaceae*, the
base numbers 6, 7, 8, 9, 10, 11, 12, 13, 14, 15 and 17 are found.
This family is divided into two sub-families, *Silenoideae* and
Alsinoideae, and in these again different degrees of cytological
heterogeneity prevail.   In the *Silenoideae*, the tribe *Lychnideae*
including the genera *Silene*, *Melandrium*, *Viscaria*, *Lychnis*,
Agrostemma, *Cucubalus*, etc., is characterised by the quite
uniform base number of 12.   In the tribe *Diantheae*, also in
this sub-family, the base numbers 14, 15 and 17 occur—for
example, 14 in the genus *Saponaria*, 15 in *Vaccaria*, *Dianthus*
and *Kohlrauschia*, and 17 in *Gypsophila*.   In the other sub-
family of the *Caryophyllaceae*, *Alsinoideae*, much greater
irregularity prevails, since base numbers of 6, 7, 8, 9, 10, 11,
12, 13, and 14 occur.   Even on this level, some degree of correlation between the morphologically based classification and
chromosome number is occasionally present, however, for
certain base numbers characterise small groups of genera, an
example being the tribe *Sperguleae*, including the British
genera *Spergula* and *Sperguiaria*, with a base number of 9.
But in other tribes, e.g. *Alsineae*, practically the whole range
of base numbers known in the family occur, and in the single
genus *Stellaria*, series are found which appear to be based
upon 8, 10, 11, 12, 13 and perhaps even higher numbers.

The buttercup family, *Ranunculaceae*, provides an example
in which karyotypic data appear to be of taxonomic value in
providing a logical basis for the redistribution of genera in
tribes.   Here, both chromosome morphology and number
give leads as to what may represent "natural" arrangements,
some of which run counter to groupings based on comparative

morphology. Since the original morphological groupings themselves have been somewhat arbitrary, the "cytological" reclassification may well give a truer indication of affinity. Again, we can take a single example to illustrate the type of evidence which has been considered relevant, and the sort of change to which it has led. In each of the two of the major tribes defined by the German systematist Engler, the *Helleboreae* and the *Anemomeae*, genera with base chromosome

Order: CENTROSPERMAE

Family: *Chenopodiaceae* $x=9$	Family: *Caryophyllaceae* $x=6, 7, 8, 9, 10, 11, 12, 13, 14, 15,$ and 17	
	Subfamily: *Silenoideae* $x=12, 14, 15$ and 17	Subfamily: *Alsinoideae* $x=6, 7, 8, 9, 10, 11, 12, 13$ and 14
	Tribe: *Lychnideae* $x=12$	Tribe: *Sperguleae* $x=9$
	Tribe: *Diantheae* $x=14, 15$ and 17	Tribe: *Alsineae* $x=6, 7, 8, 9, 10, 11, 12, 13$ and 14
		Genus: *Stellaria* $x=8, 10, 11, 12$ and 13

FIG. 11. Part of the Order *Centrospermae* as currently classified, showing how cytological data relating to base chromosome number sometimes show agreement with the morphologically based taxa and sometimes not. See text.

numbers of 7, 8, and 9 are placed, and also genera with very small chromosomes together with those possessing large ones. The genera *Aquilegia* and *Isopyrum* in the *Helleboreae* and *Thalictrum* and *Anemonella* in *Anemoneae* have in common the base number 7 and possess very small chromosomes; in recognition of this, they have been segregated in another tribe, *Thalictreae*. Another pair of anomalous genera, *Coptis* and *Zanthorhiza*, included in *Helleboreae*, have in common extremely small chromosomes and the base number 9. These have also been segregated in an additional tribe, *Coptideae*. The rearrangement leaves the original tribes much more homogeneous cytologically, and is also supported by some morphological data.

Cytological Variation at the Level of Species

It must be emphasised that in a case such as that of the *Ranunculaceae* just discussed, what is concerned is the re-arrangement of higher categories, a matter which is mainly of academic interest. In the practical sphere, as for example, in the work of a herbarium, the arrangement of tribes, etc., does not greatly signify (as long as it does not change too frequently) in that the species and genera are still recognised by their morphological attributes whether they are grouped in tribes based upon morphological *or* cytological criteria. In the study of variation at and below the level of species, cytology plays a very different role, for it becomes a source of data often of paramount importance. Much of its value in this respect has arisen from genetical work of the last few decades, for almost since it began, plant genetical research has been closely co-ordinated with studies of the chromosomes which are, after all, the physical bearers of the heredi-tary material. Because certain observable cytological pheno-mena are known to arise from or be associated with particular genetical events, it is now possible to make many important deductions from cytological preparations, even without any form of experimentation. We have already seen an example of this: evidence of reproductive peculiarities like agamos-permy is provided simply by the observation that fertile, seed-producing individuals of a species are habitually triploid. Similarly, an observation of two different chromosome numbers in two related groups would itself be sufficient to suggest that a sterility barrier exists between them, since hybrid progeny, if any were produced, would be likely to be partially or completely sterile because of meiotic irregularities which would almost inevitably arise. As a matter of fact, it is strongly argued by many cytogeneticists that all obser-vations of differences in chromosome number should be accepted as indicating "specific" distinction, because of their implication of intersterility. Formerly, it was commonly accepted that such a phenomenon as "intraspecific" polyploidy existed, and that cytologically different populations (*cytotypes* —cf. ecotypes, topotypes) could resemble each other so closely in external morphology that no distinction could be made between them. But it has become clear that when intensive morphological studies are conducted using the guide given by cytology, distinctions between races differing in chromosome number can usually be detected, even if only by statistical methods. It is interesting to note that many of the critical taxa distinguished by early taxonomists have proved to be cytologically distinct. An example is provided by the yellow bird's-nest, *Monotropa hypopythis*. On morphological grounds this has been treated either as two species or one species with two varieties, one with the inside of the flowers stiffly hairy (var. *hirsuta*) and the other hairless (var. *glabra*). It is now known that the former is a hexaploid, with $2n=48$, and the latter a diploid, $2n=16$. The current practice of retaining the hexaploid as the species *M. hypopythis* and giving specific rank to the var. *glabra* as *M. hypophegea* is thus justifiable on cytological grounds. A case where taxonomic study has so far failed to distinguish morphological groups corresponding consistently to all of the existing cytotypes is that of the lady's-smock, *Cardamine pratensis*, in which chromosome numbers of 30, 56, 58, 60, 64, 68, 76 and 84 have been found. However, there is evidence that the cytotypes have different ecological tolerances, those with higher numbers occurring in wetter habitats, and a classification into morphological groups may yet become possible.

Detection of Differences in Chromosome Structure

As we have seen, a certain amount can often be deduced about differences in chromosome *structure* in related species simply from comparison of their karyotypes. But much more can usually be learned from studies of meiotic behaviour in hybrids between them, either made artificially in the experimental garden or collected in nature. Preparations for the study of meiosis can very easily be made in some favourable groups, as for example in the lily family, *Liliaceae*, and some grass genera, simply by squeezing out and staining the contents of very young anthers when the pollen-mother cells are in course of division. In less favourable material, serial sections of young flower-buds are required. In suitable preparations, the configurations of the pairing chromosomes can be observed, and from these the degree of structural dissimilarity can often be inferred.

To see how meiotic pairing behaviour in a hybrid can sometimes reveal structural differences in the chromosomes of its parents, we may take a simplified example. Let us

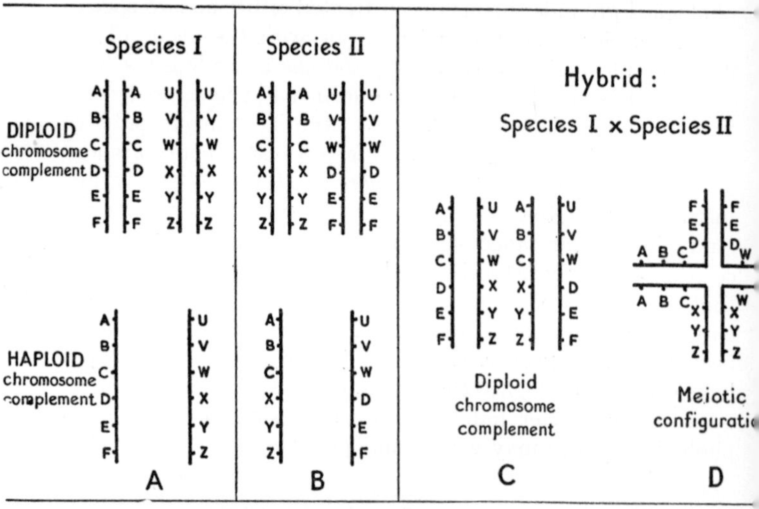

FIG. 12. Chromosome pairing behaviour in a hybrid between two species which differ in the structure of two chromosomes of the haploid set as a result of segmental interchange. For explanation, see text.

presume that two species differ in the structure of two chromosomes of the set, so that the order of the genes in species I is as in Fig. 12A, and, through exchange of equal segments, as in Fig. 12B in species II. Such an exchange would normally not be detectable by simple observation. In the hybrid between the two species, a set of chromosomes would be contributed by each parent and the diploid complement would therefore include two pairs with unlike gene arrangements as in Fig. 12c. Since no gene *changes* are involved, such a hybrid would be as well balanced genetically as its parents. However, when the pairing of early meiosis begins, corresponding gene blocks will be unable to match with each other unless a complicated figure of four chromosomes is formed, as in Fig. 12D.

Obviously if figures of this type are observed in the meiosis of hybrids, they indicate structural differences in the parental chromosomes. More elaborate structural changes than that illustrated in Fig. 12 actually do occur, and the meiotic figures they give rise to are naturally more complex, sometimes involving more than two pairs of chromosomes. Apart from translocation of parts (of which the case discussed above is an example), inversion of segments, losses and duplications are also known. In all of these cases the nature of the differences can be deduced from the configurations observed in favourable preparations.

It will be appreciated that this type of structural modification of the chromosome complement, even although it need involve no change in the genotype either in composition or quantity, must lead to a certain degree of hybrid sterility due to maldistribution of the genetical material at meiosis. Here we have the potentiality of a taxonomically rather disturbing situation, where races identical in gene make-up are nevertheless partly intersterile because of dissimilarity in chromosome structure. This has certain important implications in connection with the sterility-fertility criterion of species. Races of this nature are known, e.g., in maize, where they have actually been produced artificially, and also in many wild species. A good example is the thorn-apple, *Datura stramonium*, which occasionally occurs as a garden weed in Britain. Crosses between various races from different localities throughout the world, carried out by American geneticists, have shown meiotic configurations which suggest that translocations involving two or more chromosomes differentiate some of the races, even although they are not morphologically distinguishable except where genic differences are also present.

The occurrence of these dissimilarities in chromosome structure between different races of plants may have important evolutionary results, since by imposing partial intersterility it may supply the reproductive isolation necessary for the ecological differentiation of populations. In passing, it is worthy of note that one explanation suggested for the fixation of certain structural rearrangements in some populations, particularly segmental inversions, is that, to begin with, a favourable gene combination may be protected from disruption if it happens to occur in an inverted segment of a chromosome, since segregation of genes in this segment will not be possible in crosses with "non-inverted" individuals. The whole gene block will then be handed on intact in the hybrid progeny, leaving the possibility that it will appear in the homozygous condition in several individuals. These may be at an advantage in competition with other biotypes due to their favourable genotype, and the strain so set up, safe from disruption of its particular adaptative gene-complex, may eventually come to dominate in certain habitats.

Variation in Chromosome Number: Autopolyploidy and Allopolyploidy

Cytogenetical work has thrown a great deal of light on the ways in which changes of chromosome number can take place, and has revealed furthermore the sort of phenotypic effects which can be expected to arise from such changes. Research on the tobacco plant, *Nicotiana tabacum*, and the thorn-apple mentioned above, has shown that *loss* of a chromosome in diploids usually renders a plant inviable. In higher polyploids, because of the buffering effects of the other chromosome sets, loss may not be fatal, so that aneuploids may come into existence and perhaps even persist under some circumstances. On the other hand, the gain of an extra chromosome in the thorn-apple does not greatly affect the viability of the individual, and a series of plants has been produced experimentally in this species each with a different one of the twelve chromosomes of the haploid set present three times instead of twice. Naturally this involves genetical unbalance, and this is revealed phenotypically since every one of the series can be distinguished morphologically on the basis of fruit and other characters. A few of the possible combinations in which two chromosomes are present twice have been produced, but this amount of unbalance seriously affects the vigour and survival capacity of the plant.

Many ways in which polyploidy can arise are now known. The simplest form involves the progressive duplication of the same chromosome set, and is known as autopolyploidy. In some plants, chromosome doubling often occurs in buds regenerating from cut branches, and autotetraploids can sometimes be obtained in this way. In cereals, chromosome doubling has been provoked by temperature shocks. But the most important and generally effective way of producing polyploids is through the treatment of buds or seeds with the alkaloid, colchicine. Colchicine has the property of suspending temporarily the function of the spindle mechanism, so that during mitosis the daughter chromosomes do not separate in the normal manner to form independent nuclei. Instead, "restitution" nuclei are produced containing both daughter sets of chromosomes, so that tissues in which the number is doubled are formed. Generally speaking, autotetraploids initially show general similarity to their diploid parents, but often reveal a certain amount of gigantism in various organs, and can be distinguished by their larger cells (including, of course, pollen grains) as well as larger nuclei. Their fertility is usually also impaired, in part at least because of the tendency for groups of four instead of two chromosomes to be formed in the meiotic prophase, which usually results in maldistribution of genetical material. After a few generations of inbreeding all of these tendencies may be mitigated to some extent, and fertility may rise again.

Interesting although autopolyploidy is to the experimentalist, it does not appear that this has been the main source of the polyploids observed in nature. Experimental and other evidence has shown that many have probably arisen through the addition of dissimilar chromosome sets or genomes followed by doubling rather than through the duplication of the same one, so that they are allopolyploids rather than autopolyploids. The difference may be represented simply. Let us assume a species with a haploid genome which we can denote as A. The normal diploid plant would be AA, and a derived autotetraploid, AAAA. Assuming another species with the genome B, its diploid cells would contain BB, and its hybrid with the first species, AB. If we assume now that the hybrid were to double its chromosomes, it would become an allotetraploid, AABB. The importance of this process is that even if the original hybrid, AB, were itself sterile because of lack of homology between the A and the B chromosomes, in the allotetraploid two homologous sets would be restored due to the doubling of both the A and the B complements, and there is once again the opportunity for normal meiotic pairing and the production of viable spores. One might even expect that the more sterile the original hybrid because of the absence of homology between the A and B sets, the more fertile would be the allotetraploid through the smaller chance of pairing anomalies resulting from the association of more than two chromosomes. As a matter of fact, this inverse correlation between the fertility of the hybrid and its chromosome-doubled derivative is in practice sometimes found to exist.

Many "synthetic" allopolyploids have been produced through doubling the chromosomes of sterile hybrids by one of the available methods. But in addition it is known that many "Linnæan" species have had such an origin in nature, and one or two have even been synthesised. Well known examples are tobacco, *Nicotiana tabacum*, $2n=48$, from *N. sylvestris* and *N. tomentosiformis* each with $2n=24$, and the hemp nettle, *Galeopsis tetrahit*, $2n=32$, from *G. pubescens* and *G. speciosa* each with $2n=16$. There is one case in which a "good" taxonomic species appears to have arisen by this process in nature during the period of human observation, that of the cord-grass, *Spartina townsendii*. This species, in which $2n=126$, arose in Southampton Water by the doubling of the chromosomes of the hybrid between the European *Spartina stricta* with $2n=56$ and the introduced North American *S. alterniflora* with $2n=70$. It is reasonably fertile, very vigorous and is in places bidding fair to oust the parents. Its value as a mud-stabiliser is such that it has now been planted for this purpose in many parts of the world.

In several other taxonomic species there is excellent circumstantial evidence of allopolyploid origin, often with clear indication of one or both parents. From the large sample of species that has already been investigated it is estimated that perhaps half of the entire north temperate flora of the world consists of polyploids, and that of these, most are likely to be allopolyploids. The importance of this process of species-formation in the higher plants is thus considerable, particularly when the further fact is appreciated that very many plants which are important in agriculture have almost certainly arisen in this way.

CHAPTER VII

THE EXPERIMENTAL CATEGORIES

By the end of the nineteenth century, systematists had completed a primary survey of the plant kingdom using the classical techniques of plant taxonomy with morphology as a main source of data, and had constructed a classificatory system which was of considerable utilitarian value. This "alpha" taxonomy, as it has been termed by Turrill, provided the essential initial orientation for the new sciences—genetics, cytology, ecology, etc.—at the outset of their own explorations of the natural variation of plants. However, as new data accumulated in the various special fields, it became clear that the morphologically based units of existing alpha taxonomy did not invariably conform with the variational units which the experimental techniques revealed, and indeed that the lower categories of the taxonomic hierarchy were themselves by no means ideally adapted to accommodate the experimental units. Accordingly, various experimentalists have been impelled to construct new systems of categories to replace them, and to define these new categories with their own special criteria. We have already encountered some of the genecological units of infraspecific rank; in the present chapter we are concerned with those which are intended to accommodate variational units at and somewhat above the level of the usual Linnæan species. These categories of "experimental taxonomy" are themselves in an "experimental" stage, and there is still a good deal of disagreement as to how exactly they shall be framed. Since so much depends upon definition, it seems appropriate to commence by considering some of the definitions of the experimental categories proposed by various workers, and then proceed to a discussion of their implications.

The Systems of Turesson and Danser

Turesson's later definition of the *ecospecies*, quoted on p. 70, involved the postulate that its constituents should be freely interfertile, but that crosses between different ecospecies should give rise to "less vital or more or less sterile descendants in nature." In more concise genetical language this implies that free gene exchange is possible within ecospecies, but that under natural conditions it is impeded to some extent between different ecospecies.

In 1929, about the same time as Turesson brought the fertility-sterility criterion into genecology, a Dutch botanist, Danser, proposed a scheme of categories based upon this same criterion but with less emphasis on the ecological aspect. Danser's lowest unit was the *convivium*, a group of inter-breeding individuals distinguishable morphologically from others and geographically isolated to some extent from them*. Convivia were apparently intended to represent natural units observable in the field, which would correspond sometimes with ecotypes or topotypes, but might in some cases rank rather with ecospecies. The unit of next highest rank was the *commiscuum*, which was defined as containing all of those individuals capable of exchanging genes. This is clearly a unit which cannot be defined by observation, but only by experimental test of the capacity for gene exchange. In Danser's definition, the *facility* with which gene exchange takes place was not taken into account, and therefore the commiscuum does not correspond with Turesson's ecospecies, but is obviously of higher rank, since ecospecies are only "more or less" intersterile while different commiscua are totally incapable of gene exchange. The category of highest rank in Danser's system was the *comparium*, which was intended to include all of those plants which could be united by hybridity, whether or not the hybrids were sterile.

Turesson himself had, in 1922, proposed a higher category

*Note that the concept of the *convivium* is different from that of the *gamodeme*, for the latter need not necessarily be morphologically differentiated (see footnote, p. 28).

than the ecospecies, the *coenospecies*, which denoted ". . . the total sum of possible combinations in a genotype compound." Defined in this manner, the coenospecies is something of a hypothetical unit, and in 1929, at the time of his redefinition in genetical terms of the ecospecies, Turesson also redefined the coenospecies, as follows: "A population-complex the constituents of which group themselves in nature in species units of lower magnitude on account of vitality and sterility limits, having all, however, a common origin as far as morphological, cytological or experimental facts indicate such an origin." The coenospecies was thus transformed into a real unit, composed of "species" the properties of which conform with those of ecospecies. This definition of the coenospecies does not, however, include a positive statement of a genetical criterion for recognising them, and for this reason, it was considered to be too vague by many of Turesson's successors.

Some years later, Gregor and his collaborators introduced the criterion of total incapacity for gene exchange between coenospecies in their definition, which was as follows:

"Coenospecies: A group distinguished by morphological, physiological or cytological characters, or a combination of these; separated from all other plants by sterility or by the failure of hybrids to produce viable seed. Parts of a coenospecies may have become separated by natural barriers, e.g., oceans or mountain ranges, so that all potential hybridisations cannot occur in nature." This was combined with a redefinition of the ecospecies as: "A group also distinguished by morphological, physiological or cytological characters, or a combination thereof; separated from other parts of its coenospecies by restricted fertility or by the failure of hybrids to establish themselves in nature." Later, in 1939, Gregor simplified these definitions in a radical manner, eliminating any demand for morphological, physiological or cytological differences and any suggestion that events in nature should be taken into account. The coenospecies became: ". . . a population which is incapable of exchanging genes with other populations, even when given the opportunity," while the

ecospecies was defined as ". . . a population with an inherently low capacity for exchanging genes with other populations of its coenospecies." Similar definitions of these important categories were adopted by Clausen, Keck and Hiesey: "*Ecospecies*, all the ecotypes genetically so related that they are able to exchange genes freely without loss of fertility or vigour in the offspring. *Coenospecies*, all the ecospecies so related that they may exchange genes among themselves to a limited extent through hybridisation."

Although all of these workers have continued to accept the ecotype concept itself in the same general sense as had originally been intended by Turesson, we see that they were impelled by the need for more precision in the definition of the higher units of genecology eventually to place the entire weight for the discrimination of ecospecies and coenospecies on a genetical criterion, namely the experimental test of capacity for gene exchange.

Considering for the moment only capacities for (a) hybrid formation and (b) gene exchange (and neglecting the important problem of how these capacities are to be tested) the characteristics of the more important experimental categories of Danser and Turesson may be summarised as follows:

Unit	(a) Whether capable of hybridisation with others of similar rank	(b) Capacity for gene exchange with others of similar rank
Comparium (Danser)	no	nil
Coenospecies (Turesson)	possibly	nil
Commiscuum (Danser)	yes	nil
Ecospecies (Turesson)	yes	limited
Convivium (Danser)	yes	free to limited
Ecotype (Turesson)	yes	free

It will be appreciated that genetical criteria such as are incorporated in the definitions of Danser's categories and in the more recent redefinitions of Turesson's are in a class quite apart from any that have been used in the discrimination of orthodox taxonomic units. Although reproductive isolation may arise from morphological differences, e.g., through specialised flower structure, it is not necessarily dependent upon such differences; nor, for that matter, is it necessarily associated with cytological dissimilarities, although again it *may* arise from such a source. As was early realised by some taxonomists, experimental and otherwise, it is essentially a special criterion, and any classification which may arise from its employment must be "special" in the sense that while possessing unique properties of its own it may show no correlation whatever with others based upon different criteria.

The Significance of the Sterility-Fertility Criterion

It is, of course, on the presumption that the sterility-fertility criterion concerns a property of fundamental importance in governing the natural variation of plants that it has been given such prominence in framing genecological units. On the level of ecotypes and topotypes, it is assumed that the different populations are potentially interfertile, and that their reproductive isolation is imposed by spatial isolation alone. At the level of ecospecies, checks to gene exchange which are genetically determined are assumed to have arisen, and at the level of coenospecies, to have become complete. The existence of inherent reproductive isolation between two groups implies their genetical independence, and therefore the attainment of such isolation marks a cardinal point in the evolutionary history of diverging populations, for thereafter they can grow side by side and, within one and the same area, become the progenitors of further lines of diverging populations.

But in spite of the theoretical importance of this, it does not follow that reproductive isolation always marks the attainment of the same point in the evolutionary history of a group, or that it arises inevitably in the same manner. We have seen that all degrees of isolation may be imposed upon populations by external factors governing their distribution in space: from the very slight, such as must prevail between the populations of sea plantains at the top and the bottom of a salt-marsh to the complete, such as exists between populations of a species separated by a great ocean. We have further seen that the morphological and physiological divergence of populations inherently capable of interbreeding is normally dependent upon some degree of geographical isolation, but does not necessarily *result* from such isolation. Similarly, it appears that when geographical isolation has provided the conditions for genetical divergence, such divergence, should it occur, does not necessarily lead to the appearance of other, inherent, barriers to crossing.

In one way, of course, the fact that for genetical reasons two populations have different ecological tolerances is itself a form of inherent difference which tends to inhibit interbreeding, but it is barriers other than those which operate through imposing geographical isolation which are tested in the experimental garden. The appearance of barriers of the latter type may be delayed until long after sufficient morphological differences have accumulated to justify taxonomic recognition of two isolated populations as species, for many instances are known of species-pairs which are fully interfertile but which are well differentiated morphologically and have had a long history of geographical isolation. A classical case is that of the two plane-tree species, *Platanus orientalis* and *P. occidentalis*, the former from the eastern Mediterranean area, the latter from eastern North America. The two species are perfectly "good" taxonomically, yet the hybrid, "*P. acerifolia*," the familiar London plane, is highly fertile.

As a matter of fact, there is evidence to suggest that inherent reproductive barriers may arise far more slowly and haphazardly between spatially remote populations than between neighbouring populations undergoing differentiation. A possible explanation for this is that once ecological specialisation has begun, hybrids arising as a result of cross-pollination between individuals of the different populations would be less well adapted to the available habitats than progeny arising from pollinations within the populations, and thus less likely to survive. Should any form of isolating mechanism appear by chance, selection would thus favour its establishment, since those individuals prevented by it from hybridization would leave a greater number of viable progeny. In remote populations there would be no such premium on an isolating mechanism, since they cannot in any event influence each other by hybridization.

It is clear, then, that while some ecotypes and topotypes are likely to be incipient ecospecies, it would be erroneous to assume that all are. Looking at the matter in the reverse sense, it would appear also to be unjustified to assume that all existing ecospecies have arisen from ecotypes or topotypes which have begun their differentiation under conditions of spatial isolation. Undoubtedly some which are now vicarious, or almost so, have arisen in this manner, as probably have others possessing nowadays greatly overlapping areas which have resulted from secondary spread from separate original centres of origin. Ecospecies of this nature have had an *allopatric* origin, having arisen originally in spatial isolation. But it seems that many plants which must rank as ecospecies on the basis of the genetical criterion have had no such origin, but have come into being through the occurrence of auto- or allopolyploidy or other radical chromosomal or genic changes which have involved the immediate appearance of a reproductive barrier between them and their parents growing in the same area. Such an origin is termed *sympatric*.

If the experimental test of interfertility is made the sole criterion of what shall be taken as ecospecies, then not all of the units discriminated as such can be expected to be biologically equivalent. Some units will be relatively minor, like the numerous cytotypes of *Cardamine pratensis*, mentioned in the previous chapter, which, differing as they do in chromosome number, must necessarily show a degree of reduced fertility in crosses and therefore qualify as ecospecies if the purely genetical criterion is adopted. Similarly, the races of *Datura stramonium*, although morphologically indistinguishable, nevertheless show partial intersterility and could therefore also be regarded as ecospecies.

In contrast, we find that just as a rigid application of the experimental test of interfertility would tend to discriminate forms as ecospecies which would hardly qualify as such on Turesson's original basis, so it would tend to deny ecospecific rank to forms which would appear from their behaviour *in nature* to have every claim to the rank. As we have seen, ecological and morphological differentiation of populations does not predicate intersterility. Apart from cases like that of the two *Platanus* species quoted above in which geographical separation has been a long-term isolating factor, there are many morphologically quite distinct taxonomic species which are maintained apart in nature largely by *ecological* factors and which, because of their interfertility, would be reduced to mere ecotypes by strict application of the fertility-sterility criterion. The example of the genus *Quercus* in North America has already been mentioned. Familiar cases in the British Isles are the two species of *Geum*, *G. urbanum*, wood avens, and *G. rivale*, water avens, and the two species of *Melandrium*, *M. rubrum*, red campion, and *M. album*, white campion; each of these pairs shows high interfertility in experimental crossing. Nevertheless, the taxonomic species concerned have much of the character of ecospecies in the original Turessonian sense, since they only exceptionally exhibit their interfertility in the field through the formation of hybrid-swarms, and then mostly as a result of human interference. It was no doubt to preserve the claim of these and similar groups to "ecospecific" rank that Turesson laid emphasis on what happened "in Nature" in his later definition of the ecospecies, which was actually illustrated by the example of the *Geum* species mentioned above.

That the sterility-fertility criterion does not necessarily discriminate equivalent biological units in different alliances does not, of course, invalidate its use for the production of a special classification. It must, however, be recognised that such a classification need not have direct relevance to the situation in the field, since in some cases the criterion upon which it is based tests something which is never tested in the field, while in others the results it gives are of little more than academic interest because they are over-ruled in practice by the operation of factors which it does not take into account.

Practical Difficulties in the Interfertility Test

Although there is theoretical justification for attempting to construct classifications of populations on the basis of their fertility inter-relationships, a serious drawback arises in the practical application of experimental tests, in that it is difficult to know how far the experimenter is justified in intervening to bring about crossing between plants in culture. By growing plants together, the isolating effects of spatial separation are circumvented. But what other bars to crossing are to be removed artificially? If artificial pollination is adopted, then all those which depend upon selective or assortative pollination by insects are removed, even although they are genetically determined and thus "inherent" and fully effective in the field. Even if the usual precaution of ensuring that no other pollen reaches the stigma than that under test is adopted, such perfectly good "inherent" isolating factors as pollen-tube competition are eliminated. The test then comes down to a check on hybrid viability and fertility. But even this can never really be positive, for different results may be obtained under different culture conditions, as has already been revealed in practice by contradictory reports from different workers ostensibly testing the same species. Furthermore, there is the important fact that a single test between two "representative" biotypes does not always prove the case for the *populations* involved, whether its results are negative or positive. Others from different sources may show totally different degrees of interfertility.

It is also noteworthy that the actual effort involved in carrying out all of the controlled crossings required to prove whether all of the ecotypes of a single species were not, in fact, ecospecies in respect to each other, or that all of the races of two ecospecies were equally isolated, would in many cases prove so enormous that for practical reasons no more than a fraction of the tests could be carried out.

Generally speaking, the practice has been to perform some of the more obvious crossings and then to work from these by analogy, relying mainly for guidance upon morphological resemblances and dissimilarities.

The Coenospecies and the Comparium

The coenospecies, the highest rank of the original system of Turesson, differs according to recent definitions from the ecospecies in that its members are totally incapable of gene-exchange with those of other coenospecies. In theory, at least, the experimental tests which are made to distinguish populations which can be adopted as ecospecies must also eventually define the coenospecies to which they belong. When a crossing between two forms is made which is totally unsuccessful, or which produces totally sterile hybrids, then a boundary of the coenospecies may have been reached. But if both can exchange genes with a third form, they and the third form must be reckoned as belonging to the same coenospecies. Presumably, the chain could be even longer than three links. This reveals that the coenospecies, as defined by the genetical test, is likely to embrace taxonomic units of very different size in different groups. Some coenospecies are naturally small and easily definable, containing perhaps one ecospecies, which may correspond to one taxonomic species isolated morphologically and possibly phylogenetically from others. Again, through some genetical freak, a total sterility barrier may have developed around one or two not otherwise particularly well distinguished species of a genus, which accordingly must be separated from the remainder in a different coenospecies. From the results of crossings which have been reported, such total sterility barriers apparently surround some species of the foxglove genus, *Digitalis*, and of *Geum*. It seems not impossible that a single race of a taxonomic species, regarded perhaps as no more than a sub-species or variety on morphological grounds, should under some circumstances have become totally isolated reproductively and so rank as a coenospecies. Recent work on the genus *Clarkia* suggests that this situation may actually be approached in one Californian species, where one particular local population has been found to be almost completely isolated reproductively from all others with which it has so far been tested.

In contrast, it seems that the coenospecies in some alliance would be enormously large. Crossing experiments have shown that in some large genera no reproductive barriers exist at all, and horticultural experience in the field of orchid breeding suggests that in some tropical sections of this family the coenospecies would embrace four or five *whole genera*.

With the category of coenospecies, we have reached the ceiling for direct genetical investigation of the structure of plant populations, since genetical study demands breeding experiments, and by definition coenospecies cannot be crossed or produce sterile hybrids. The unit which embraces all of those coenospecies which can be crossed through any of their members to produce viable hybrids corresponds to the *comparium* of Danser. It should be noted that the comparium marks the theoretical level beyond which the evolutionary history of different lineages must become finally independent. The coenospecies does not mark such a level, for different coenospecies, although incapable of gene exchange, may produce hybrids, and these while initially sterile may regain fertility by chromosome doubling. The genomes of ecospecies from different coenospecies may thus be added in allopoly-ploids with the potentiality of further evolutionary development.

Proposals for a Unified system of Category Terminology

It will be evident from the above discussion that the terminology of experimental categories is not at present too satisfactory, firstly, because there are competing systems in the field, and secondly, because different workers have interpreted the more widely used terms in rather different senses. There is now a proposal for a unified scheme of category nomenclature, based upon Gilmour's and Gregor's "deme" terminology (mentioned on p. 28). It is suggested that this could form a base upon which a system of terms could be constructed having reference to populations possessing definable genetical, cytological or other characteristics. The proposed root—"deme" in all compounds would simply imply —"one or more populations of the taxon under discussion." Some of the first-order derivatives originally proposed by Gilmour and Gregor have already been mentioned, namely gamodeme, ecodeme and topodeme. Others would be *genodeme*, a population differing genetically from others; *cytodeme*, a population differing in some distinctive cytological feature from others. Among important second-order derivatives would be *ecogenodeme*, a population differing genetically from others which occupies a specific ecological habitat, i.e. an ecotype in Turesson's sense. In sexual plants, the ecogenodeme would be composed of one or more gamodemes. The sum of all gamodemes between which free gene-exchange could take place if the opportunity were provided (e.g. in the experimental garden) would be a *hologamodeme*, which would then be the equivalent of the ecospecies as interpreted by Gregor and others. Correspondingly, the sum of those hologamodemes between which restricted amounts of gene-exchange is possible directly or indirectly would be a *coenogamodeme*, a unit equatable with the coenospecies as interpreted by recent workers. Coenogamodemes capable of linkage by the formation of sterile F_1 hybrids would collectively form a *syngamodeme*, which would be equivalent to Danser's comparium.

8

CHAPTER VIII

THE RELATIONSHIPS OF " EXPERIMENTAL " AND " ORTHODOX " TAXONOMY

THE preceding chapter will have served to show that the approach to organic variation embodied in what is often loosely termed "experimental" taxonomy differs in a great many respects from that of the "classical" taxonomy as practised, for instance, in museums and herbaria up to the beginning of the present century. The extent and nature of the differences may be summed up as in the table on pages 108, 109.

It will be seen from this table that these two disciplines differ in methods, and what is more important, in their fundamental aims. It is not difficult to see why this should be so. Attempts at systematic classification of the plant kingdom began in the first instance because of the necessity of reducing to some sort of order the extreme diversity of *form* which was apparent in it, and it was in this manner that classical taxonomy acquired its primary and unchallengeable aim of describing, naming, cataloguing and classifying all living plants on the basis of their morphology. It deals with organisms as they exist in the present, and must moreover make the assumption that its units have some degree of permanence. It has no direct concern with evolutionary *processes*, although what it deals with are the products of evolution, and although some of its results may be interpreted as a form of representation of evolutionary events. In direct contrast, "experimental" taxonomy is actually in large part the study of evolution itself. A synthesis of several experimental sciences, it is concerned with analysis of existing patterns of variation mainly with a view to determining the evolutionary processes which brought them into being. Classical taxonomy is all-embracing, claiming the whole plant kingdom as its sphere. The field of experimental taxonomy is at present limited to the relatively few groups amenable to its methods and to those to which its results can be applied by analogy; its "ceiling" is the level at which genetical experimentation becomes impossible, so that in actuality no chance of producing an all-embracing classification based upon experimental methods exists at all.

Almost as important as the divergence of aims is the fact that orthodox taxonomy has perforce to employ comparative morphology (including comparative anatomy) as its primary data source, for this is the only one which can be called upon with reasonable facility throughout the plant kingdom. Degrees of morphological difference must remain the principal indication of "relationship" in most groups, and the *general* system of classification must be based upon these, irrespective of the fact that genetical and other criteria may be claimed as superior in some small alliances.

The special field of "experimental" taxonomy

For these reasons it has been the view of many experimental taxonomists, particularly those who have also had experience of the operation of great general herbaria, that no attempt should be made to introduce fundamental modifications of the structure of orthodox taxonomy to allow it to assimilate the new concepts in their entirety, especially where changes of basic criteria would be involved. They recognise that the experimental concepts influence (and, at least for the time being, can influence) only small parts of the field with which taxonomy has to deal, and that the change of attitude they would engender in those parts would lead to incongruity and an undesirable variation of practice from alliance to alliance according as to whether the caprice of experimenters had or had not led them into this or that group. Taxonomists who take this view advocate that experimental "classifications" should be given complete freedom to develop along whatever

"EXPERIMENTAL" TAXONOMY

AIMS

To identify evolutionary units, and by experiment to determine their genetical inter-relationships and the role of the environment in their formation.

UNIT OF STUDY

In non-sexual organisms, the biotype; in sexual organisms, the breeding population or large representative sample of it. Material preferably living.

SYSTEM OF CLASSIFICATION

Classification as such is not a primary aim; where classifications are produced they are intended mainly to present in a systematic fashion data which have been obtained about natural populations. The *basic units* adopted are diverse, according to immediate purpose and the system in use; e.g. ecotypes, topotypes, convivia.

Taxonomic structure. No general system is adopted, but in some groups minor hierarchies have been constructed to reflect the genetical relationships between populations. None of these extends upwards beyond the level at which genetical experimentation becomes impossible.

SOURCE OF DATA

Inherent in the plants (*a*) from dead material: morphology, anatomy, karyology; (*b*) from living material: observation of complete life cycles; study of physiological behaviour and morphological adaptation in different habitats; genetical tests of interfertility; cytological studies aimed at establishing breeding-systems, etc.

Non-inherent. Geographical distribution, ecology.

TESTS OF CHARACTERS

Observational techniques using statistical methods; experimental techniques using transplanting to test phenotypic variability, and controlled crossings to determine modes of inheritance.

METHODS OF DESCRIPTION

Based upon populations or population samples, using statistical methods. Nomenclatural matters considered of little importance.

CONCEPT OF NATURAL VARIATION INVOLVED

Essentially *dynamic*. Full weight is given to the importance of the genetical systems (i.e. breeding behaviour) operative in the groups under study. No rigid "species concept" is accepted or required. The internal variability of sexual populations is recognised, and the adaptative nature of much population differentiation is acknowledged and made a deliberate object of study. Classification is based upon evolutionary units where these can be recognised and is not committed to a set of formal categories. No general classification of the plant kingdom is attempted.

"CLASSICAL" TAXONOMY

AIMS

To describe all existing "kinds" of plants, to classify them according to their resemblances and differences, and to name them according to a body of internationally agreed rules.

UNIT OF STUDY

Individuals or small numbers of individuals, usually dead.

SYSTEM OF CLASSIFICATION

Basic unit. The "species," which is accepted as having objective reality (originally because of the dogma of special creation, and later through the interpretation of evolution as simply another word for "the origin of species").

Taxonomic structure. A hierarchy of categories embracing the whole of the plant kingdom and named according to internationally agreed rules.

SOURCE OF DATA

Inherent in the plants (a) determinable from dead material: external morphology, later internal morphology (anatomy); (b) from living material: little taken into account except features like periodicity (flowering time, deciduousness, etc.)

Non-inherent. Geographical distribution.

TESTS OF CHARACTERS

Intuition (based on accumulated experience) and trial and error.

METHODS OF DESCRIPTION

Based upon individuals and the "type" concept.   The giving of names accepted as an important process.

CONCEPT OF NATURAL VARIATION INVOLVED

Essentially *static.* Assumes continuity of form within species, except for a small amount of "sporting" and variation between individuals. The adaptative significance of differences between plants is not taken into account. The taxonomic hierarchy is accepted as a suitable form of representation of natural variation, and its application in the internationally agreed form is regarded as obligatory in all groups. Higher units than species are based exclusively upon degrees of morphological resemblance or dissimilarity, although phylogenetic ideas have led to the construction of putative character series intended to show lines of descent.

lines prove suitable, to incorporate such data as experimental-ists may desire, and not to be obliged in any way to relate themselves either to the grouping or nomenclature of orthodox taxonomy. If this attitude is taken, since the experimental classifications are avowedly independent, it does not matter in the least that their categories should fail to correspond with the orthodox taxonomic ones—that coenospecies, for example, should in one alliance incorporate only a single taxonomic species or subspecies, and in another four or five whole genera. Each form of grouping is based upon its own criteria, and each is equally valid.

Another salutary effect would be to discourage experimental workers from using their results to support far-reaching taxonomic revisions of groups in which they happen to be working, and particularly regroupings which, on the basis of an artificial genetical test, would cut right across widely accepted and otherwise unchallenged arrangements based upon comparative morphology. But it would not prevent the arrangement of such units as may be detected in experi-mentation in specifically "experimental" categories so as to summarise what is known about them and their inter-relation-ships, and in such a manner that the connections with orthodox taxonomic classifications can be grasped immediately.

The Expansion of Orthodox Taxonomy

Naturally, the proposal that the special classifications of "experimental taxonomy" should be built up independently employing their own criteria does not imply that orthodox taxonomy can dismiss the new ideas about natural variation as irrelevant and ignore altogether the genetical, cytological, physiological, ecological and other research of the last half century. Many taxonomists have come to recognise that a certain amount of reorientation on the basic philosophical level, as well as modification—in some places, radical—of practice, has become obligatory. They hold to the legitimacy of the aims of orthodox taxonomy, and acknowledge the practical value of the existing taxonomic structure. But they realise that this structure should be accepted for what it is —a formal representation of the variation of plants using a conventionalised system of categories and nomenclature.   If this is recognised, the danger of assuming that the whole of the taxonomic system is, or can be, a "projection" of evolution is avoided.   Moreover, it becomes obvious that all natural variation cannot be expected to fit neatly into the formal taxonomic framework, widely applicable although it has proved to be. A great variety of causes lies behind the variation observable in different plant groups, and it is therefore patently futile to suppose, as did many taxonomists of the nineteenth century, that *all* groups *must* be amenable to treatment by defining and naming "species" if only we were competent to detect the real lines of demarcation.

At the same time, there has been increasing realisation that even if no suggestion of replacing the original basic criteria can (as yet, anyway) be entertained, the implications of the new work must be taken into account in bringing up to date taxonomic procedure and in framing, defining and describing the units of orthodox taxonomy.   In preceding chapters, attention has been drawn repeatedly to experimental findings which reflect directly upon taxonomic practice.   The most important relate to such matters as:

(a) the variability in phenotypic expression of the individual genotype;

(b) the genetical basis of morphological differences, quantitative variation and character correlation;

(c) the diversity of breeding systems in flowering plants, and their paramount importance in governing group variation;

(d) the local breeding population as the unit of importance in sexual species, and methods of describing and defining its structure;

(e) the different possible biological meanings of population differentiation within species;

(f) the occurrence of clinal variation and methods of studying it, and

(g) the causes and consequences of natural hybridisation.

Most of these factors concern variation at and below a level corresponding roughly with the Linnæan species, and they therefore affect principally the lower ranks of the taxonomic hierarchy. Of recent years there has been much discussion as to how these can be adapted to fill the new requirements. Naturally, most attention has been paid to the "species" category itself, since it is quite clear that for the purposes of *classification*, quite apart from any deeper biological meaning which may attach to the concept of species, there must be a degree of agreement as to what use is going to be made of this category of the taxonomic hierarchy. Several taxonomists have put forward definite proposals as to the different types of populations which can logically be fitted into it in groups where different genetical systems and different degrees of regional and ecological variation prevail, and have attempted to show how the infra-specific categories allowed for in the international rules governing nomenclature* can be put to more consistent and rational use. A theoretical analysis of some possibilities was provided some time ago by the Swedish taxonomist and ecologist, du Rietz, and while much of experimental taxonomy has developed since he wrote in 1930, his

*The International Code of Botanical Nomenclature, which is revised at intervals by the International Botanical Congresses, is concerned with setting out the formal structure of the taxonomic system and the principles which will be adopted in nomenclature. It is not concerned directly with defining the types of natural units which will be fitted into the various categories, but with the order of these categories in the hierarchy and the names which will be applied to them. The species (Latin, *species*) is adopted as the basic category, and within it the categories recommended for general use are, in descending sequence, subspecies (*subspecies*), variety (*varietas*) and form (*forma*). Provision is made for recognising special physiological races (*formae speciales*), hybrid segregates (*nothomorphae*) and apomicts (*formae apomictae*).

proposals remain of importance since they indicate what has been, to some extent, a trend of orthodox taxonomy.

Du Rietz began with the common-sense proposition that for the purposes of taxonomy the various units have to be treated simply as concrete populations, irrespective of the possible abstract nature of the concepts involved. The problem of importance is then ". . . the definite or arbitrary nature of the borderlines between the populations accepted as units." This leads to a species concept based upon the "principle of discontinuity" in natural variation; the view accepted by du Rietz being that species must be delimited by the lines or zones of discontinuity found in nature, without taking into account the size of the unit so circumscribed, either in relation to the number of individuals or internal polymorphy. This led him to a general definition of *species* as—". . . the smallest natural populations permanently separated from each other by a distinct discontinuity in the series of biotypes . . ." Because of the different situations present in different alliances du Rietz expected that among sexual plants some species defined in this manner would be small units, showing no regional differentiation (homofacial) and others relatively large, with several regional facies (heterofacial). For such regional races he advocated retention of the term *subspecies*, the formal definition being ". . . a population of several biotypes forming a more or less distinct regional facies of a species." It was not required that subspecies populations should be sharply delimited from each other (if so, according to definition they would rank as species) but that they should intergrade more or less continuously, or be only statistically discriminable. It *was* required that they should occupy an appreciable part of the species area: i.e. that the description "regional" should be fitting. Otherwise they would rank as mere *varieties*, which were defined as populations of one or several biotypes forming a more or less local facies of a species. Morphologically marked biotypes or groups of biotypes not forming distinct geographical facies were to be ranked as *forms*.

Fundamental to these proposals of du Rietz is the postulate now accepted by most systematists that taxa must be framed around natural populations and not around some fortuitously selected specimen. More recently, two American taxonomists, Camp and Gilly, have developed this point of view in advocating an expansion of orthodox taxonomy in what they term "biosystematy." They accept the need for retention of the basic criterion of comparative morphology, but urge that it cannot be effectively applied without taking experimental findings into account. Like du Rietz, these workers lay stress on the fact that species can hardly be fashioned so as all to contain similar amounts of internal genetical variability, and base their concepts on two primary considerations:

(1) the appearance of species populations in the field, and,

(2) the genetic systems operative within these populations.

Application of these criteria leads them to recognise that at least twelve different kinds of populations are likely to qualify for inclusion in the taxonomic species category, and to these they apply descriptive Greek terms. It is not necessary here to go into the details of all of Camp and Gilly's "kinds" of species, but one or two of the more important or interesting may be quoted in illustration. The reader will no doubt recognise the situations to which they refer.

Homogeneon: a species which is genetically and morphologically homogeneous, all members being interfertile (the "ideal" taxonomic species!)

Rheogameon: a species composed of segments of reasonably marked morphological divergence whose distributions are such that gene interchange may take place in sequence between them; individuals of contiguous segments are interfertile (cf. Rassenkreis, p. 63).

Phenon: a species which is phenotypically homogeneous but which is composed of intersterile segments (cf. *Datura*, p. 89).

Dysploidion: a species composed of morphologically similar members of a dysploid series, the individuals of which are sexually reproductive (cf. *Cardamine pratensis*, p. 87).

Cleistogameon: a species which, in part, reproduces by means of cleistogamy (cf. *Epipactis*, p. 33).

All of the above kinds of species are sexual; for the groups where apomixis prevails, Camp and Gilly define two others: the *apogameon*, a species containing both apomictic and non-apomictic individuals, and the *agameon*, a species consisting of only apomictic individuals.

Camp and Gilly's treatment of the "species problem" forms another example of the taxonomist's approach to taxonomy, in that it represents an attempt to group, classify and name different kinds of species. However, these authors indicate that in proposing a group of terms to cover some of the types of population which can be given recognition as taxonomic species, they intend these as a general guide to assist systematists, and not as additions to official taxonomic terminology. They do not adopt any of the terms of experimental taxonomy, since they consider that some of the concepts implied by these terms may not be considered compatible with the production of what they call "functional systematics", i.e. systems of classification operable in museums, herbaria and the like.

In dealing with infraspecific categories, Camp and Gilly adopt a position somewhat similar to that of du Rietz. They affirm support for the present general trend to define subspecies of sexual species on the combined basis of morphological differentiation and geographical distribution, as "segments of appreciable size in relation to the entire species population which are separated from each other by definable differences in both morphology and distribution," but consider that the term might be adopted also to designate sympatric segments of species which are genetically or cytologically discriminable, provided that this is combined with some degree of morphological differentiation. They prefer to abandon the term *variety*, but retain the term *form* in its useful and fairly conventional meaning to cover variant individuals which occur intermixed with those of the species, not possessing a separate distribution.

Common to the proposals of du Rietz, Camp and Gilly

and others of recent years is the assertion that distribution as well as morphological resemblances and dissimilarities must be taken into account in framing the lower taxonomic units and this is, of course, understandable from what has been said in Chapter III about the variation of sexual organisms. If in amphimictic plants the unit of evolution is indeed the local breeding population (the *gamodeme*) there is a powerful argument for making it also the unit of classification, and for avoiding the formation of any taxa (except perhaps at the very lowest ranks, to embrace groups of distinctive biotypes within gamodemes, in the sense of du Rietz's and Camp and Gilly's "forms") which embrace parts of breeding units, or arbitrarily cut across several. If this principle is adhered to, then geographical-ecological considerations are automatically introduced, since taxa will then be composed of one or more gamodemes and this will usually mean that they will possess independent geographical or ecological distributions.

Acceptance of the gamodeme as the working unit implies that in sexual plants taxa will be defined with greatly differing amounts of internal variability, since some breeding populations are more variable than others. Correspondingly, if discontinuity of variation is made a criterion for deciding when populations are to receive recognition as separate species, the "gaps" between species may be found to vary very greatly even within the same alliance. Most taxonomists seem now to be prepared to accept these principles, even although they imply that within a single alliance two biotypes differing markedly from each other may have to be placed in the same taxon because they belong to the same breeding population, while, on the other hand, two differing to a far lesser extent may have to be placed in different taxa because of the dissimilarity of the breeding populations to which they belong.

The Problems of "Critical" Groups

In general, "critical" taxonomic groups are either :

(a) those in which lines of discontinuity along which taxa

can be shaped are indistinct because of incomplete differentiation or through hybridisation, or

(b) those in which reproductive peculiarities have produced minor groupings of biotypes which, although they are distinct enough in minor characters, embarrass the taxonomist because of their vast numbers and small amount of differentiation.

In the case of groups of the former type, there can be no doubt that what du Rietz terms the "morphological-geographical" method can often provide the means of salvation in establishing a truer picture of variation in nature. In some polymorphic groups, difficulties arise in deciding on the levels of differentiation which shall be accepted as meriting the different taxonomic ranks. This is, of course, no more than another aspect of the arbitrary nature of the taxonomic hierarchy itself, with its inherent requirement that lines of division shall be found even where no clear ones exist. Du Rietz's "species" criterion—". . . the smallest natural populations permanently separated from each other by a distinct discontinuity in the series of biotypes" is, of course, far from absolute, since although there may theoretically be a definite level below which there is "overlapping" of biotypes and above which there is none, in critical sexual groups the difficulty in species definition is simply that no such level can in practice be found which is acceptable to all specialists concerned. Furthermore, the possibility that "species" defined by this criterion might, in their areas of contact, be connected by zones in which hybridisation takes place and intermediate individuals and populations occur, means that the distinction between them and geographically intergrading regional subspecies is a very fine one indeed. Similarly, at a lower level in du Rietz's hierarchy, the limits of "subspecies" and "variety" must be set more or less subjectively, since all intermediate sizes of populations occur between those which are merely "local" and those which are "regional."

In some critical sexual groups where hybrid populations often appear to be as extensive as any which can be looked upon as "pure", the morphological-geographical method may, on its own, have very little more success in defining acceptable taxa than the purely subjective "type" method of earlier taxonomists. Situations such as these probably arise where populations which have formerly become partly differentiated in isolation have been brought into extensive breeding contact through ecological changes, and they exist in several groups in the Northern Hemisphere within the area affected by the glaciation, as well as in floras like that of New Zealand, already mentioned in this connection. Much can be learnt about these situations from statistical studies of character correlation and tests of breeding behaviour to determine which forms segregate in the manner of hybrids and which do not, but these weapons hardly belong in the armoury of orthodox taxonomy. Groups like these no doubt must remain "black spots" as far as the latter is concerned, to be covered by one or two rather wide and arbitrarily framed species descriptions and left for treatment in detail by experimental taxonomists with their different criteria.

The existence of inherent reproductive barriers between closely allied forms is a further factor which may prevent the effective application of the morphological-geographical method in delineating and defining taxa. From the purely taxonomic point of view, there is every justification in retaining within the same "species" morphologically inseparable gamo-demes which are nevertheless isolated reproductively from one another; the genetically compound species so formed would rank as a "phenon" in Camp and Gilly's system. Logically, when morphological differentiation is also present, there should be no reason for giving the segments any higher taxonomic rank because of their reproductive isolation than their degree of dissimilarity would itself warrant, but no doubt if the necessary breeding evidence were available, taxonomic practice would be swayed to take it into account and to rank the divergent segments as "species". More dis-turbing situations, however, are likely to arise where reproduc-tively isolated populations have overlapping distributions and are only slightly differentiated morphologically. Outside of the area of overlap, they may be recognisable as subspecies (and even justify specific rank if the reproductive isolation is taken into account as an ancillary criterion) but within it they may form a heterogeneous assemblage in which biotypes of one cannot be distinguished with assurance from those of the other.

This sort of situation also arises in groups in which cleisto-gamy or habitual self-pollination prevails. Here, if the discontinuity-of-variation principle is applied, "species" are likely to be defined which sometimes contain one biotype and sometimes a group of closely similar biotypes, and none may have very much significance where self-pollination is only facultative.

The extreme form of reproductive aberration, apomixis, poses one of the most excruciating of taxonomic problems. We have seen that the practice of most taxonomists who have handled these groups has been, up till recent years, to name every recognisable form as a species, and there can be no doubt that this was no more than the logical outcome of the application of the "classical" species concept. It is also the policy which rigid application of the du Rietzian principles would suggest. Other propositions have come from various sources, but none appears yet to have the potentiality of general application. Turesson has suggested that in those instances where a cluster of apomictic biotypes forms a morpho-logical assemblage which can be defined reasonably well, this group might be taken as forming a unit on par with poly-morphic sexual species, and for it he proposes the term *agamo-species*. As an example, he quotes the common lady's mantle, *Alchemilla vulgaris*; the common dandelion, *Taraxacum officinale* would be another instance. The apomictic clones within the agamospecies (if such are delimited) Turesson proposes to call simply *formae apomictae*. Critics have pointed out the impossi-bility of applying this concept in alliances where no real vari-ational foci can be detected among the apomicts, and where the next highest unit would be the genus or subgenus. In a few groups in which experimental and taxonomic studies have been combined and the sexual species from which the apomictic complex has arisen have been identified with some certainty, the possibility is open for shaping biologically significant and taxonomically acceptable groupings. American workers on the apomictic complex in the hawk's-beard genus, *Crepis*, have reached a point where this has become possible, and have produced a classification in which most of the apomicts are grouped with a relatively small number of sexual species, within or about whose variational spheres they lie. This is an approach generally similar to that adopted by some European students of the genus *Rubus*, who, although without experimental evidence, have sought to introduce some sort of rational order into what would otherwise be simply a vast morass of independent, named, forms, by grouping the apomictic "microspecies" around certain geographically widely distributed "circle-species" with which they seem to have general affinity.

The Outlook

It has been possible in this monograph to cover only a few of the more important of the new concepts which have entered taxonomy in recent years and to provide no more than a general impression of the reactions they have produced. Very little has been said about taxonomic problems above the levels affected directly by recent experimental work, and so matters such as the place of phylogenetic speculation in classification have received little consideration. However, enough ground has been covered to show how it has come about that alongside "alpha" taxonomy in recent decades the new experimental taxonomy has grown up, with its different aims and methods. It is worth noting that this new biological discipline is perhaps in a way not a form of "taxonomy" at all since the production of *classifications* is no part of its basic aims. The classifications of experimental taxonomy are summaries of facts about natural populations concerned with their structure and genetical inter-relationships as they bear upon evolutionary processes operative or formerly operative within them. It has been suggested that this type of classification may not serve much purpose, since it does not possess the practical value of orthodox classification, nor is it certain that the study of evolution is itself advanced by defining this or that sort of category. Recently, there has been a tendency among more radically minded evolutionists to deplore the "taxonomic" attitude in their science—the attitude which seeks to detect, define and classify "types," be they "eco-", "topo-", "cyto-" or of other form, rather than to study processes. Looking past the conflict of categories which has proceeded in the field of experimental taxonomy, we may perhaps glimpse a future in which the defining of categories has been abandoned altogether, and experimental study of natural variation proceeds without "typification." It is the belief of many botanists that the latter process should be left to an expanded but not wholly revolutionised taxonomy, itself a direct descendant of that of Linnæus and de Candolle, retaining its classical aims, but adapting and modifying its methods to absorb new data as they come to light. It is encouraging, at least, to hope that such a development might take place, towards what Turrill has termed an "omega" taxonomy, which could perhaps become an epitome of a very large part of human knowledge about plants.

GLOSSARY

For definitions and discussions of the experimental categories, ECOTYPE, ECOSPECIES, COENOSPECIES, CONVIVIUM, COMMISCUUM and COMPARIUM, the reader is referred to Chapter VII).

Adaptation, Any morphological or physiological character which may be assumed to increase the fitness of an organism for a particular habitat or mode of life. The process of becoming adapted. Hence ADAPTATIVE.

Agamospermy, The production of seed by asexual means.

Allelomorph, One of a pair or series of dissimilar genes which can occupy a particular position (locus) in a chromosome.

Allopatric, Originating in or occupying different geographical regions.

Allopolyploid, A polyploid originating through the addition of unlike chromosome sets.

Amphimixis, Reproduction which involves a sexual process.

Anatomy, (The study of) the internal structure of organisms.

Aneuploid, A polyploid possessing a chromosome number which departs somewhat from being an exact multiple of the base number of the series.

Apomixis, Any means of reproduction, including vegetative propagation, which does not involve a sexual process.

Assortative Breeding, Breeding which is not random, some matings being more probable than others. Usually implies fertilisation of like by like.

Autopolyploid, A polyploid originating through the multiplication of the same chromosome set.

Autosegregation, A form of segregation of genetical factors assumed to take place in some apomictic lineages, producing a certain amount of diversity in the offspring.

Auxin, A general term for the naturally occurring plant growth substances.

Back-crossing, The mating of a hybrid with one or both of its parents or parental stocks.

Base Number, The haploid or gametic chromosome number in the lowest member of a polyploid series, or sometimes what is presumed to have been this number when the species possessing it is actually unknown or extinct.

Binomial, A name consisting of two Latin words, the first the name of the genus, the second the specific epithet.

Biotype, A collection of individuals which are genotypically all essentially the same.

Cell, The constructional unit of all living things except the most elementary; composed in plants of a mass of protoplasm surrounded by a wall, containing one or more nuclei and other solid, liquid or gaseous inclusions.

Chromosome, One of the deeply staining bodies into which part of the nuclear material condenses during division.

Cleistogamy Self-pollination within an unopened flower.

Cline, Any variational trend in space appearing in a population or series of populations of a species.

Clone, A group of independent organisms derived vegetatively (i.e. without a sexual process) from a common ancestor.

Critical Group, A variable group of related organisms within which it is difficult to detect and define units suitable for taxonomic recognition.

Cytogenetics, The combined cytological and genetical study of organic variation.

Cytology, The study of the cell.

Cytoplasm, The protoplasm of the cell outside of the nucleus.

Cytotaxonomy, Classification of plants by reference to karyotypic resemblances and differences.

Cytotype, A plant or group of plants distinguished by some cytological feature from others of the species.

Deme, A population of a taxon (see the section, p. 105, dealing with this terminology for further details, and also derivatives).

Development, The qualitative changes involved in the passage of the individual organism from the zygote to the reproductive stage. Contrast GROWTH.

Dioecious, With male and female flowers on different individuals.

Diploid, Possessing two complete sets of chromosomes (thus genomes), as in the zygote and the organism which arises from it, one set contributed by each of the two parents.

Dysploid, (a) Of a series of related species, implying that their chromosome numbers do not form or approach a polyploid series consisting of exact multiples of a base number; (b) of an individual cell or plant, implying that its chromosome number departs markedly from the normal but is not an exact multiple of it.

Ecad, A form showing adaptation to a particular habitat in which the adaptative characters are not genetically determined but are imposed by environmental agencies.

Ecocline, A cline which can be associated with an ecological trend or gradient.

Ecology, (The study of) organisms in relation to their environments.

Ecophene, See ECAD.

Embryo, The young organism in the earliest stages of its development.

Euploid, A polyploid possessing a chromosome number which is an exact multiple of the base number of the series.

Extraclinal, of ecotypes and topotypes, signifying that they do not contribute to a cline.

Facies, The general aspect of a plant or population of plants.

Fertilisation, The fusion of the male and female sex-cells (gametes).

Gamete, One of the uninucleate cells, carrying each a haploid set of chromosomes, which undergo fusion to produce the zygote in the normal course of sexual reproduction.

Gametophyte, A plant producing gametes; in flowering-plants, the product of the germination of the spores, i.e. the pollen grain and the embryo sac.

Genes, The materia units of inheritance, assumed to be arranged in linear order in the chromosomes. The gene of formal genetics corresponds to the Mendelian factor; its "particulate" character is established by the fact that it represents the minimum distance between possible points of crossing-over between the chromatids of paired homologous chromosomes at meiosis. The gene defined thus is not necessarily the unit of physiological function.

Genecology, The study of the genetical structure of plant populations in relation to their habitats.

Gene-exchange, A short-hand genetical term referring to the capacity of two organisms to mate and produce more or less fertile offspring which in turn can produce more or less fertile progeny in which new combinations of the original parental genes may appear.

Genetics, The study of variation, heredity and evolution.

Genetic, Genetical, Due to or concerned with inheritance.

Genome, A single complete set of chromosomes (or genes).

Genotype, The hereditary constitution of the individual.

Growth, The irreversible increase in size of an organism without necessarily any change in the character of the cells, tissues and organs produced (contrast DEVELOPMENT).

Habitat, The total external environment of the plant.

Haploid, Possessing one single complete set of chromosomes (thus one genome) per nucleus, as in the spores, gametophytes and gametes of higher plants.

Heredity, The transmission from generation to generation of the capacity for developing corresponding attributes.

Hermaphrodite, With stamens and carpels in the same flower.

Heterostyly, Possessing styles of one length (relative to the stamens) in the flowers of some plants and different lengths in those of others of the same species.

Heterozygote, An individual arising from the fusion of gametes bearing different genomes.

Histogram, A form of graph in which classes of events or observations are indicated along a horizontal axis, and the frequency of the events or observations falling in each class by rectangles of proportionate height.

Homology, Direct equivalence of structures or organs in the same or different organisms, due to common descent.

Homologous Chromosomes, Those which associate in pairs in the first phase of meiosis, being corresponding members of haploid sets derived from the parental gametes.

Homozygote, An individual arising from the fusion of gametes bearing identical genomes.

Hormone, A chemical substance produced by some cells of the organism which regulates the activities of others.

Hybrid, (a) Taxonomically, a cross between different taxa; (b) genetically, a cross between any two forms differing genotypically.

Hybrid Segregate, A form arising in the second or subsequent generation after hybridisation.

Hybrid-swarm, A population which has arisen through the hybridisation of genetically different groups, containing first and later generation hybrids and back-crosses, and often showing great morphological variability.

Intraclinal, Of ecotypes and topotypes, signifying that they form part of a cline.

Introgressive Hybridisation, Genetical modification of one species by another through the intermediacy of hybrids.

Karyotype, The chromosome set as seen at mitotic metaphase.

Linkage, The tendency for certain characters to be inherited together, due to the presence of the genes controlling them in the same chromosome.

Meiosis, or Reduction Division, The form of nuclear division associated with the formation of the reproductive cells. It consists essentially of two divisions of the nucleus accompanied by only one division of the chromosomes, which results in reduction of the chromosome number from the diploid somatic number to the haploid gametic number. The important events are: (a) the pairing of homologous chromosomes of the diploid set point for point along their length (synapsis) to produce a haploid number of pairs; (b) the longitudinal duplication of the paired chromosomes so that each consists of two chromatids, making a total of four in association; (c) the occasional exchange of partners between the two pairs of chromatids, the places where the exchange takes place being presumably points where chromatid breakage has occurred followed by cross-fusion, i.e. crossing-over; (d) the separation of the chromatids in pairs and their passage to the poles (end of the first meiotic division); (e) the second meiotic division, in which the paired chromatids at each pole separate, move apart and reform nuclei as in a normal mitosis. These events leave a total of four nuclei, in each of which the chromosome number is half of that in the original parental nucleus, i.e. each of which carries one complete haploid chromosome set or genome. Each of these genomes is likely to be different from either of those which came together in the zygote from which the parent arose because of the exchange of corresponding chromatid segments resulting from the crossing-over mentioned above, and the subsequent random distribution of the compound chromatids so formed to the four daughter nuclei. See also LINKAGE, RECOMBINATION and SEGREGATION.

Meristic Variation, Variation in the numbers of organs or parts.

Mitosis, The form of nuclear division which occurs in somatic tissues. The complete cycle involves:

(a) The longitudinal doubling of the chromosomes in such a manner that the hereditary material which they bear is exactly duplicated in each daughter, known at this stage as a chromatid;

(b) movement of the paired chromatids so that one specific region, the spindle attachment region, lies near the equatorial plane of the cell, the stage known as metaphase;

(c) the separation of the daughter chromatids, one of each pair proceeding to a different end of the parent cell, the stage known as anaphase;

(d) the reorganisation of two new and exactly similar daughter nuclei from the two sets of chromatids (now chromosomes), the stage known as telophase.

Monoecious, With stamens and ovaries in separate flowers but on the same plant.

Morphogenesis, The origin and development of form.

Morphology, (The study of) the shape and form of organisms.

Mutation, The instantaneous origin of a heritable variation, the most important kinds being:

    (a) a change of a gene to an allelomorph;

    (b) a change in chromosome structure, involving the loss, gain, translocation, or inversion of a segment;

    (c) a change in chromosome number.

Natural System, A system of classification which groups plants so as to place together those with the maximum possible number of attributes in common.

Normal Distribution, The form of frequency distribution likely to be found when a variate is influenced by numerous independent factors all of the same order of magnitude. The mathematical properties of this distribution are well known, and much statistical theory refers to it. Since it is an empirical fact that many natural frequency distributions are roughly normal, the variation of natural populations can often be treated mathematically by fitting normal curves.

Nucleus, A body present in most living cells, formed from the chromosomes at the end of mitosis, and in the period between divisions, controlling the majority of the life processes of the cell.

Panmixis, Random breeding, in which any individual is potentially capable of mating with any other.

Perennial, Persisting for several years.

Phenotype, The organism as observed, resulting from the interaction of genotype and environment.

Photoperiodism, The response of plants to the relative lengths of day and night.

Phylogeny, The evolutionary history of groups of organisms.

Physiology, (The study of) the life processes and functions of organisms.

Polygenes, Genes with small individual effects which are assumed to co-operate in numbers to produce certain types of quantitative genetical variation.

Polymorphism, The occurrence of several distinct forms of a species in a single habitat.

Polytopic, Having come into being independently in more than one locality.

Polytypism, The occurrence of several distinct forms of a species in different parts of its range (see Rassenkreis).

Polyploid, An individual having more than two complete sets of chromosomes per cell, or a cell containing more than two sets of chromosomes.

Polyploid Series, A series of related plants in which there is an arithmetic progression of chromosome numbers. In referring to its members, the level of polyploidy is indicated by a prefix attached to the root "—ploid", which, strictly, is meaningless except in this connection.

Thus *triploid* (with 3x the base number), *tetraploid* (4), *pentaploid* (5), etc.

Population, In biology, any group of individuals considered together because of a particular spatial, temporal, or other relationship.

Propagule, Any structure which, becoming detached from the mother plant, serves as a means of propagation.

Pure Line, A lineage of individuals all originating from a single homozygous ancestor.

Ramet, In higher plants, an individual belonging to a clone.

Rassenkreis, "Circle of races"—a polytypic species in which distinct races replace each other in geographical succession.

Recombination, The sequel to segregation in meiosis, when new haploid genomes are formed through reassortment of parts of the original parental genomes. See SEGREGATION.

Reproductive Isolation, The separation of two groups of organisms from each other, by any means, so that they cannot interbreed.

Restitution Nucleus, A nucleus formed from all of the chromosomes present in a cell following the failure of a division.

Rhizome, A root-like underground stem.

Satellite, A small, often almost spherical segment set off from the end of a chromosome by a constriction.

Segregation, The separation at meiosis of the members of homologous gene pairs.

Sexual System, The classification devised by Linnaeus which was based upon the number and distribution of the essential organs of the flower, viz., the stamens and carpels.

Somatic, Referring to the vegetative part of an organism as apart from the reproductive structures.

Somatic Mutation, A mutation occurring in vegetative tissues.

Species, One of the categories of taxa recognised in the International Code of Botanical Nomenclature, that to which a binomial is given. In this book the word is used to refer to units which have been given such recognition, or which are of a character which would justify such recognition. Some other categories of taxa recognised in the International Code are listed on p. 114.

Statistics, The branch of mathematics which treats of variation.

Stolon, A sucker or runner.

Sympatric, Originating in or occupying the same geographical region.

Synapsis, The pairing of the homologous chromosomes of the diploid set in the early stages of the first meiotic division.

Syngamy, The fusion of the gametes; fertilisation.

Systematics, The practice of describing, naming and classifying living things.

Taxon, A classificatory unit of any rank.

Taxonomy, (a) In a general sense, the science of classification; (b) in biology, the study of the principles, practice and results of the classification of organisms.

Transplanting, The transfer of part or all of a living plant from one locality to another. TRANSPLANT, the plant so transferred.

Trinomial, A name consisting of three Latin words, the first the name of the genus, the second referring to the species and the third to the subspecies.

Topocline, A geographical variational trend which is not necessarily correlated with an ecological change.

Topotype, A more or less isolated population showing genetical differences from others which cannot be correlated with ecological differences.

Type specimen, The individual of a species to which the original specific name must remain attached in any taxonomic revision. The nomenclatural type system is intended to promote stability and consistency in naming; it does not suppose that a species or other taxon can adequately be described by reference to the type specimen.

Variate, In a statistical study, the measurement (dimension, weight, etc.) the variation of which is under investigation.

Vicarious Species (Races, etc.), Closely related forms which occupy neighbouring geographical areas, i.e., "replace" each other geographically.

Vivipary, Propagation by the production of small bulbils or plants in the place of seeds or flowers.

Zygote, The product of union of two gametes; the first cell of the diploid individual.

SUGGESTIONS FOR FURTHER READING

ANDERSON, E. 1949; "Introgressive Hybridisation." Wiley.

CAMP, W. H. and GILLY, C. L. 1943; "The Structure and Origin of Species," Brittonia, Vol. 4, p. 323.

DAVIS, P. H. and HEYWOOD, V. H. 1964; "Principles of Angiosperm Taxonomy," Oliver & Boyd Ltd., Edinburgh and London.

GREGOR, J. W. 1944; "The Ecotype." Biological Reviews of the Cambridge Philosophical Society, Vol. 19, p. 20.

HESLOP-HARRISON, J. 1960; "Infraspecific Differentiation," Planta Medica, Vol. 8, p. 208.

1962; "Purposes and Procedures in the Taxonomic Treatment of Higher Organisms." Symposia of the Society for General Microbiology No. 12, "Microbial Classification," p. 14.

1963; "Species Concepts: Theoretical and Practical Aspects." In "Chemical Plant Taxonomy," p. 17, Academic Press, London and New York.

1964; "Forty Years of Genecology." In "Advances in Ecological Research," p. 160. Academic Press, London and New York.

HIESEY, W. M. 1940; "Environmental Influence and Transplant Experiments," Botanical Review, Vol. 6, p. 181.

HUXLEY, J. S. (Editor) 1941; "The New Systematics," Oxford.

STEBBINS, G. L. 1950; "Variation and Evolution in Plants," Oxford University Press, London.

TURESSON, G. 1922; "The Species and Variety as Ecological Units," Hereditas, Vol. 3, p. 100. "The Genotypical Response of the Plant Species to the Habitat," Hereditas, Vol. 3, p. 211.

TURRILL, W. B. 1938; "The Expansion of Taxonomy, with Special Reference to the Spermatophyta" Biological Reviews, Vol. 13, p. 342.

1946; "The Ecotype Concept. A Consideration with Appreciation and Criticism, Especially of Recent Trends," New Phytologist, Vol. 45, p. 34.

1948; "British Plant Life," Collins, London.

DU RIETZ, G. E. 1930; "The Fundamental Units of Biological Taxonomy," Svensk Bot. Tidskrift, Vol. 24, p. 333.

INDEX

ADAPTATION, of transplants, 22-26
  of populations, 46-56
Agameon, 115
Agamospecies, 119
Agamospermy, 31, 86
Agrostemma, 84
Agrostis canina, 72, *tenuis*, 72
Åkarp, Sweden, 47-48
Alchemilla vulgaris, 119
Alchornea ilicifolia, 31
Alpine rockcress, see *Arabis petraea*
Alps, 20
Alsinoideae, 84-85
Amphibious bistort, see *Polygonum amphibium*
Amphibious plants, 24
Amphimixis, 28
Anemone, 85
Anemonella, 85
Aneuploidy, 81, 90
Anderson, E., 78
Apogameon, 115
Apomixis, 30-32, 43, 115, 119-120
Aquatic plants, 24, 29, 61
Aquilegia, 85
Arabis petraea, 60
Archieracium, 47
Asclepiadaceae, 73
Australia, flora of, 77
Autosegregation, 31
Avens, see *Geum*
Avinlochan, 61-62

BAUHIN, K., 6
Bent grass, see *Agrostis*
Binomial system, 6
Biosystematy, 114
Biotype, 28
Bird's-foot trefoil, see *Lotus*
Blackberry, see *Rubus*
Bladder campion, see *Silene cucubalus*
Breeding systems, 37-38, 40, 42

British Ecological Society, 23
Bonnier, G., 21-22, 46-47

CALIFORNIA, altitudinal transect, 22, 51-52
Calluna vulgaris, 21
Camp, W. H., 114-116, 118
Campion, red and white, see *Melandrium*
Canadian pondweed, see *Elodea canadensis*
Candolle, A. P. de, 1-3, 7, 45, 121
Cardamine pratensis, 87, 100, 114
Carex divisa, 81, *hirta*, 81
Caryophyllaceae, 84-85
Categories, taxonomic, 6, 68, 113; terminology of, 105
Cell differentiation, 15
Centaurea nemoralis, 23; *nigra*, 77; *jacea*, 77
Centrospermae, 84
Character correlation, 3
Chenopodiaceae, 84-85
Chromosomes, 13; morphology of, 79, 81-82; number, 79-81; structure, 87-90
Circle of races, see Rassenkreis
Circle-species, 120
Clarkia, 104
Classification, 1-2, 14, 98, 101, 106, 121
Clausen, J., et al., 50-54, 58, 97
Cleistogamy, 32-33, 119
Cleistogameon, 115
Clements, F. E., 22, 49
Cline, 54, 68
Clone, 18; formation in nature, 29
Coenospecies, 96-98, 103-104, 110
Colchicine, 91
Commiscuum. 95, 97
Comparium, 95, 97, 103-104, 105
Convivium, 95, 97
Coptideae, 85
Coptis, 85

Coral root, see *Dentaria bulbifera*
Cord-grass, see *Spartina townsendii*
Crataegus, 32
Creation, special, 4-5
Crepis, 120; *capillaris*, 83; *aspersa*, 83, *capillaris* × *aspersa*, 83
Critical groups, 10-11, 116
Cross pollination, 32-33
Cryptogams, 9
Cucubalus, 84
Cytodeme, 105
Cytology, 11, Chap. VI
Cytotype, 87

DANDELION, see *Taraxacum officinale*
Danser, B. H., 95, 97, 105
Darwin, C., 8-10
Datura stramonium, 89, 101, 114
Day length, 17
Deme, 28; -deme, 105
Dentaria bulbifera, 29
Developmental plasticity, plant and animal, 14-15
Devil's-bit scabious, see *Succisa pratensis*
Diantheae, 84-85
Dianthus, 84
Digitalis, 104; *purpurea*, 39
Dioecism, 39
Discontinuity of variation principle, 10, 113, 116, 119
Du Rietz, E., 113-117
Dysploidion, 114

ECAD, 49
Ecocline, 54-55, 58
Ecodeme, 28, 105
Ecogenodeme, 105
Ecology, 12
Ecological gradient, 54-57
Ecophene, 49
Ecospecies, 69-70, 95-98, 100-101, 103; allopatric and sympatric origins of, 100
Ecotype, 48, 58, 69, 95, 97-98, 100, 103, 105
Elodea canadensis, 29
Engler, 85
Epilobium angustifolium, 22; *latifolium*, 22

Epipactis, 33, 114; *helleborine*, 33; *atropurpurea*, 83
Erophila verna, 45
Euploidy, 81
Evolution, 4, 8-9
Experimental cultivation, 44-46

Fagaceae, 82
Fescue, see *Festuca*
Festuca vivipara, 30
Fertility, 25
Form (forma), 115-16
Formae apomictae, 112, 120
Foxglove, see *Digitalis purpurea*

Galeopsis pubescens, 93; *speciosa*, 93; *tetrahit*, 93
Galium verum, 21
Gamodeme, 28, 53, 94, 105, 116, 118
Gene, 13-14; exchange, 28, 67, 76, 97; segregation and recombination, 28, 38
Genecology, 46
Genetical drift, 39, 53, 62
Genetics, 11
Genodeme, 105
Genome, 3, 92; disharmony, 73-74
Genotype, 13-15, 19, 24
Geum, 104; *urbanum*, 101; *rivale*, 101
Geographical variation, 59-67
Gilmour, J. S. L., 28, 105
Glück, H., 24
Gramineae, 30
Gregor, J. W., 28, 53-55, 58, 68, 96
Gypsophila, 84

HAWKWEED, see *Hieracium*
Hawthorn, see *Crataegus*
Heather, see *Calluna vulgaris*
Helianthemum chamaecistus, 21; *grandiflorum*, 21
Helleboreae, 85
Helleborine orchis, see *Epipactis helleborine*
Heredity, 11

Heterophylly, 24
Heterostyly, 39
Hieracium, 11, 32; *umbellatum,* 48-49, 53, 58; f. *filifolium* (oecotypus *arenarius*), 58
Hiesey, W. M., see Clausen et al.
Histogram, 34
Hologamodeme, 105
Homogeneon, 114
Horticultural plants, 29
Huxley, J. S., 54
Hybrid-swarm, 76-77, 101

ICE AGE, 59
Infraspecific categories, 113-114, 116
International Code of Botanical Nomenclature, 66, 112
Introgressive hybridisation, 78
Isolating mechanisms, 70
Isolation, 56; reproductive, 69-76
Isopyrum, 85

JOHANNSEN, W., 32
Jordan, A., 45
Jordanon, 45
Juniper, see *Juniperus communis*
Juniperus communis, 21

KARYOTYPE, 79, 81-84
Keck, D., see Clausen et al.
Knapweed, see *Centaurea*
Kohlrauschia, 84

LADIES' BEDSTRAW, see *Galium verum*
Lagopus scoticus scoticus, 63; *L.s. hibernicus,* 63
Lamarck, J. B., 2
Light environment, 17
Liliaceae, 88
Lindley, J., 4-5, 8. 70
Linnæus, C., 2-3, 6-7, 10, 121
Linneon, 45
London plane, see *Platanus acerifolia*
Lotsy, J. P., 45
Lotus alpinus, 21; *corniculatus,* 21
Lychnideae, 84-85
Lychnis, 84

Lysimachia vulgaris, 46
Lythrum salicaria, 39

Maianthemum bifolium, 65; *canadense,* 65
Maize, 89
Marsden-Jones, E. M., 23
Massart, J., 24, 44
May lily, see *Maianthemum*
Meadow rue, see *Thalictrum*
Mean, 36
Melandrium, 84; *album,* 101; *rubrum,* 58, 101, var. *crassifolium* (oecotypus *salinus*), 58
Mendel, J. G., 11
Mertensia alpina, 22; *lanceolata,* 22; *pratensis,* 22; *sibirica,* 22
Microspecies, 120
Microtopotype, 68
Modification (environmental), 44, 48-50
Monotropa hypopithys var. *glabra,* 87, var. *hirsuta,* 87; *hypophegea,* 87
"Morphological - geographical" method, in taxonomy, 117-118
Mutation, 60; somatic, 13, 28
Mountain ash, see *Sorbus aucuparia*

NATURAL SELECTION, 9, 60
Natural system, 3, 5, 7-8
New Zealand, flora of, 77, 118
Nicotiana sylvestris, 92, *tabacum,* 92, *tomentosiformis,* 92
Nomenclature, 6; of categories, 105
Non-adaptative differentiation, 59
Normal distribution, 36, 42
Nuclear division, 13
Nucleus, 13, 14; restitution, 91
Nuphar americanum, 65; *luteum,* 65
Nymphaea alba, 61; *occidentalis,* 62

OAK, see *Quercus*
Ophrys apifera, 72, *muscifera,* 72

Orchid, see *Orchis*; bee, see *Ophrys apifera*; fly, see *Ophrys muscifera*; spotted, see *Orchis maculata, O. fuchsii*

Orchis fuchsii, 41, 65-66, 75, 83, subsp. *fuchsii*, 65-66, *hebridensis*, 65; *maculata*, 65, 75, subsp. *ericetorum*, 67, 75, 83

Oxalis acetosella, 65; *montana*, 65

PERENNATING ORGANS, 17
Phenon, 114, 118
Phenotype, 13, 20, 24; phenotypic plasticity, Chap. II.
Photoperiodism, 17
Phylogeny, 8, 120
Physiology, 11; physiological processes, 16-17
Pikes Peak, Colorada, 22
Plantago major, 23; *maritima*, 53-54, 58, 68-69, 99
Plantain, see *Plantago*
Platanus, 101; × *acerifolia*, 99; *occidentalis*, 99; *orientalis*, 99
Pollination, assortative, 72; mechanisms, 71-73
Pollinia, 73
Polygenes, 40
Polygonum amphibium, 24, 44
Polymorphism, 39
Polyoecism, 39
Polyploidy, 74, 80; allo- and auto-90-93; intraspecific, 87
Pondweed, see *Potamogeton*
Populations, 27-28; adaptation of, 46; differentiation of, 44-45, 59-60; internal variability of, Chap. III; non-sexual, 33-37; panmictic, 28, 37
Potamogeton, 29
Potato, see *Solanum tuberosum*
Potentilla glandulosa, 51-53, 58, subsp. *nevadensis*, 58, subsp. *reflexa*, 58, subsp. *typica*, 58
Potterne, Wilts., 23
Primrose, see *Primula vulgaris*
Primula vulgaris, 39
Princess bean, 32-33
Pure line, 32

Purple loosestrife, see *Lythrum*
Pyrenees, 20

Quercus, 73, 101

RAMET, 18
Ranunculaceae, 84-86
Rassenkreis, 63, 114
Reproductive isolation, 69, 98, 118-119; breakdown of, 75
Rheogemeon, 114
Rockrose, see *Helianthemum chamaecistus*
Rose-bay willow-herb, see *Epilobium angustifolium*
Rubus, 11, 17, 32, 34, 42, 80, 121; *incurvatus*, 19

Salix, 11, 43; *atrocinerea*, 80, *myrsinites*, 80, *phylicifolia*, 80, *viminalis*, 80
Salt marshes, 49
Saponaria, 84
Satellites, 81
Saxifrage, 25
Self pollination, 32-33, 119
Sewall Wright effect, 39, 54
Sex balance, 17, 25
Sexual system, 2-3
Sierra Nevada, 22, 51
Silene, 84, *alpina*, 21, *cucubalus*, 21
Silenoideae, 84-85
Smith, J., 31
Soil influences, 23
Solanum tuberosum, 30
Sorbus americana, 66; *aucuparia*, 66
Southampton Water, 93
South Uist, 61-62
Spartina alterniflora, 93; *stricta*, 93, *townsendii*, 93
Speciation, 11
Species, 2, 4-5, 10, 113; category, 112-114; constancy, 4-5; interconversion of, 21-22; Lindley's definition of, 4; pairs, 65-66, 99 problem, 43, 115; relict, 59-60
Spergula, 84
Spergularia, 84

Sperguleae, 84-85
Sporogenesis, 74
Standard deviation, 36
Statistics, 36
Stellaria, 84-85
Sterility-fertility criterion, 69, 89, 97-101
Subspecies, 113, 115, 119
Succisa pratensis, 49

Taraxacum officinale, 35-37, 80, 119
Taxon, 27
Taxonomy, 1-2; classical, Chap. I, 106-110; experimental, 45, 94, 105, 108, 110, 119-20; zoological, 63
Thalictreae, 85
Thalictrum, 85
Thorn apple, see *Datura stramonium*
Tobacco, see *Nicotiana*
Tolerance range, 21, 26
Topocline, 55, 68
Topodeme, 28, 105
Topotype, 68, 95, 98, 100
Tournefort, P., 3
Transplanting experiments, 16, 18-23, 45, 52
Trinomials, 63
Turesson, G., 44-48, 54, 58, 69-70, 95-97, 101

Turrill, W. B., 23, 77, 94, 121
Type method, 68, 118, 120-121, nomenclatural, 66

Vaccaria, 84
Variation, geographical, Chap. V; meristic, 36; quantitative, 34-37 40-41
Variety, 113, 115
Vegetative reproduction, 28-29
Viburnum alnifolium 65, *lantana*, 65
Vicarism, 63
Viola, 32
Viscaria, 84
Vivipary, 30

WATER LILY, white, see *Nymphaea;* yellow, see *Nuphar*
Wayfaring tree, see *Viburnum*
Whitlow grass, see *Erophila verna*
Willow, see *Salix*
Wood sorrel, see *Oxalis*

YELLOW BIRD'S NEST, see *Monotropa*
Yellow loosestrife, see *Lysimachia vulgaris*

Zanthorhiza, 85
Zygote, 13-14